Slowly
Does It...

Good Housekeeping

Slowly
Does It...

COLLINS & BROWN

First published in the United Kingdom in 2014 by
Collins & Brown
10 Southcombe Street
London
W14 0RA

An imprint of Anova Books Company Ltd

The Good Housekeeping website is
www.goodhousekeeping.co.uk

10 9 8 7 6 5 4 3 2 1

ISBN 978-1-909397-14-9

A catalogue record for this book is available from
the British Library.

Reproduction by Dot Gradations Ltd, UK
Printed and bound by 1010 Printing International Ltd, China

This book can be ordered direct from the publisher. Contact the marketing
department, but try your bookshop first.

www.anovabooks.com

Recipes in this book are taken from the Good Housekeeping recipe library and
may have been reproduced in previous publications.

Picture Credits

Photographers:
Neil Barclay (pages 42, 46, 47, 56, 57, 58,
61, 87 and 98); Martin Brigdale (pages 51,
113, 156 and 212); Nicki Dowey (pages 6,
12, 13, 15, 16, 17, 19, 20, 21, 22, 24, 25,
27, 28, 33, 37, 38, 45, 50, 59, 65, 73, 75,
81, 89, 94, 99, 100, 104, 106, 108, 109,
110, 112, 117, 118, 124, 129, 134, 138,
141, 143, 145, 146, 152, 155, 158, 161,
162, 163, 166, 168, 170, 172, 175, 176,
177, 179, 181, 183, 185, 187, 188, 191,
193, 195, 196, 197, 201, 203, 207, 209,
215, 217, 219, 220 and 236); Will Heap
(page 149); Fiona Kennedy (pages 43, 93
and 137); Gareth Morgans (pages 67, 69,
71 and 97); Craig Robertson (pages 8, 9,
11, 30, 31, 52, 64, 74, 79, 84, 86, 90, 95,
101, 105, 123, 127, 128, 133, 140, 147,
151, 153, 165, 167, 171, 182, 198, 202,
205, 206, 211, 224, 225, 226, 227, 228,
229, 230, 231, 232, 233, 234 and 235);
Maja Smend (pages 115 and 132); Clive
Streeter (page 40); Lucinda Symons (pages
35, 55, 62, 82, 91, 99, 103, 119 and 121);
Kate Whitaker (page 131).

Home Economists:
Anna Burges-Lumsden, Joanna Farrow,
Emma Jane Frost, Teresa Goldfinch, Alice
Hart, Lucy McKelvie, Kim Morphew, Aya
Nishimura, Katie Rogers, Bridget Sargeson,
Sarah Tildesley, Kate Trend, Jennifer White
and Mari Mererid Williams.

Stylists:
Susannah Blake, Tamzin Ferdinando,
Wei Tang, Sarah Tildesley, Helen Trent and
Fanny Ward.

Notes

Both metric and imperial measures are given for the recipes. Follow either set of measures,
not a mixture of both, as they are not interchangeable.
All spoon measures are level.
1 tsp = 5ml spoon; 1 tbsp = 15ml spoon.
Ovens and grills must be preheated to the specified temperature.
Medium eggs should be used except where otherwise specified.

Dietary Guidelines

Note that certain recipes contain raw or lightly cooked eggs. The young, elderly, pregnant
women and anyone with immune-deficiency disease should avoid these because of the slight
risk of salmonella.
Note that some recipes contain alcohol. Check the ingredients list before serving to children.

Contents

SOUPS

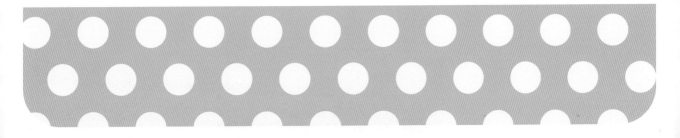

Simple Vegetable Soup

Preparation Time 15 minutes • Cooking Time 50 minutes • Serves 4 • Per Serving 96 calories,
6g fat (of which 1g saturates), 8g carbohydrate, 0.2g salt • Vegetarian • Gluten Free • Dairy Free • Easy

1 or 2 onions, finely chopped

**2 tbsp oil or 1 tbsp oil and 25g (1oz)
butter**

**1 or 2 garlic cloves, crushed
(optional)**

**450g (1lb) chopped mixed
vegetables, such as leeks,
potatoes, celery, fennel, canned
tomatoes and parsnips, chopped
finely or cut into larger dice for a
chunky soup**

1.1 litres (2 pints) vegetable stock

1. Fry the onions in the oil or oil
and butter until soft and add the
garlic, if you like.

2. Add the chopped mixed
vegetables and the stock. Bring to
the boil, then reduce the heat and
simmer for 20–30 minutes until the
vegetables are tender.

3. Leave chunky, partially purée or
blend until smooth.

Summer Vegetable Soup with Herb Pistou

Preparation Time 20 minutes • Cooking Time 1 hour • Serves 6 • Per Serving 163 calories, 7g fat (of which 1g saturates), 17g carbohydrate, 0.1g salt • Vegetarian • Gluten Free • Dairy Free • Easy

3 tbsp sunflower oil

1 onion, finely chopped

225g (8oz) waxy potatoes, finely diced

175g (6oz) carrots, finely diced

1 medium turnip, finely diced

4 bay leaves

6 large fresh sage leaves

2 courgettes, about 375g (13oz), finely diced

175g (6oz) green beans, trimmed and halved

125g (4oz) shelled small peas

225g (8oz) tomatoes, seeded and finely diced

1 small broccoli head, broken into florets

salt and ground black pepper

pistou (see Cook's Tip) or ready-made pesto to serve

1. Heat the oil in a large pan over a gentle heat. Add the onion, potatoes, carrots and turnip and cook for 10 minutes. Pour in 1.7 litres (3 pints) cold water, season with salt and pepper, bring to the boil and add the bay and sage leaves. Reduce the heat and simmer for 25 minutes.

2. Add the courgettes, beans, peas and tomatoes. Bring back to the boil and simmer for 10–15 minutes. Add the broccoli 5 minutes before the end of the cooking time.

3. Remove the bay and sage leaves and adjust the seasoning. Pour the soup into warmed bowls and serve immediately; serve the pistou or pesto separately to stir into the hot soup.

COOK'S TIP

Pistou is a Provençal condiment similar to Italian pesto.

To make your own, using a pestle and mortar or a small bowl and the end of a rolling pin, or a mini processor, pound together ¾ tsp sea salt and 6 chopped garlic cloves until smooth. Add 15g (½oz) freshly chopped basil and pound to a paste, then mix in 12 tbsp olive oil, a little at a time. Store in a sealed jar in the fridge for up to one week.

Roasted Tomato & Pepper Soup

Preparation Time 20 minutes • Cooking Time about 1 hour • Serves 6 • Per Serving 239 calories, 16g fat (of which 6g saturates), 15g carbohydrate, 0.4g salt • Gluten Free • Easy

1.4kg (3lb) full-flavoured tomatoes, preferably vine-ripened
2 red peppers, seeded and chopped
4 garlic cloves, crushed
3 small onions, thinly sliced
20g (¾oz) fresh thyme sprigs
4 tbsp olive oil
1 tbsp Worcestershire sauce
4 tbsp vodka
salt and ground black pepper
6 tbsp double cream to serve

1. Preheat the oven to 200°C (180°C fan oven) mark 6. Put the tomatoes into a large roasting tin with the red peppers, garlic and onions. Scatter 6 thyme sprigs over the top, drizzle with the oil and roast in the oven for 25 minutes. Turn the vegetables over and roast for a further 30–40 minutes until tender and slightly charred.

2. Put one-third of the vegetables into a blender or food processor with 300ml (pint) boiled water. Add the Worcestershire sauce and vodka and then season with salt and pepper. Whiz until smooth, then pass through a sieve into a pan.

3. Whiz the remaining vegetables with 450ml (¾ pint) boiled water, then sieve and add to the pan.

4. To serve, warm the soup thoroughly, stirring occasionally. Pour into warmed bowls, add 1 tbsp double cream to each bowl, then drag a cocktail stick through the cream to swirl. Scatter a few fresh thyme leaves over the top and serve immediately.

Autumn Vegetable Soup

Preparation Time 15 minutes • Cooking Time 45 minutes • Serves 4 • Per Serving 326 calories, 17g fat (of which 9g saturates), 29g carbohydrate, 1.1g salt • Easy

50g (2oz) butter
1 medium onion, diced
450g (1lb) potatoes, diced
100g (3½oz) diced bacon
1 garlic clove, chopped
100g (3½oz) white of leek, chopped
2 Cox's Orange Pippin apples,
   unpeeled, cored and chopped

2 tsp dried thyme
1 tsp dill seeds (optional)
600ml (1 pint) dry cider
900ml (1½ pints) hot vegetable
   stock
125g (4oz) Savoy cabbage leaves,
   shredded
salt and ground black pepper

1. Melt the butter in a large pan, then add the onion, potatoes, bacon, garlic, leek, apples, thyme and dill seeds, if using. Season to taste with salt and pepper, stir, then cover the pan and cook gently for 15 minutes.

2. Add the cider and bring to the boil, then reduce the heat and simmer for 5 minutes. Add the hot stock and simmer for about 15 minutes or until the potatoes are soft.

3. Pour half the soup into a blender or liquidiser and whiz until smooth, then add to the remaining soup in the pan. Reheat gently, add the shredded cabbage and simmer for a further 3 minutes. Ladle into warmed bowls and serve.

Green Lentil & Coconut Soup

Preparation Time 20 minutes • Cooking Time 40 minutes • Serves 4 • Per Serving 442 calories,
22g fat (of which 10g saturates), 48g carbohydrate, 0.3g salt • Vegetarian • Dairy Free • Easy

225g (8oz) whole green lentils
4 tbsp sunflower oil
350g (12oz) floury potatoes, diced
1 large onion, chopped
2 garlic cloves, crushed
¼ tsp ground turmeric
2 tsp ground cumin
50g (2oz) creamed coconut

750ml (1¼ pints) vegetable stock
300ml (½ pint) coconut milk
finely grated zest of 1 lemon
salt and ground black pepper
toasted fresh coconut and
**   coriander sprigs (optional) to**
**   garnish**

1. Put the lentils into a sieve and wash thoroughly under cold running water. Drain well.

2. Heat the oil in a large pan. Add the potatoes and fry gently for 5 minutes or until beginning to colour. Remove with a slotted spoon and drain on kitchen paper.

3. Add the onion to the pan and fry gently for 10 minutes or until soft. Add the garlic, turmeric and cumin and fry for 2–3 minutes. Add the coconut, stock, coconut milk and lentils and bring to the boil, then reduce the heat, cover the pan and simmer gently for 20 minutes or until the lentils are just tender.

4. Add the potatoes and lemon zest and season to taste with salt and pepper. Cook gently for a further 5 minutes or until the potatoes are tender. Ladle into warmed bowls, garnish with toasted coconut and the coriander sprigs, if you like, and serve hot.

Pepper & Lentil Soup

Preparation Time 15 minutes • Cooking Time 45 minutes • Serves 6 • Per Serving 165 calories, 3g fat (of which 1g saturates), 27g carbohydrate, 0.5g salt • Vegetarian • Dairy Free • Easy

1 tbsp oil
1 medium onion, finely chopped
1 celery stick, chopped
1 leek, trimmed and chopped
1 carrot, chopped
2 red peppers, seeded and diced
225g (8oz) red lentils
400g can chopped tomatoes
1 litre (1¾ pints) hot light
   vegetable stock
25g pack flat-leafed parsley,
   chopped
salt and ground black pepper
toast to serve

1. Heat the oil in a pan. Add the onion, celery, leek and carrot and cook for 10–15 minutes until soft.

2. Add the red peppers and cook for 5 minutes. Stir in the red lentils, add the tomatoes and hot stock and season to taste with salt and pepper.

3. Cover the pan and bring to the boil, then reduce the heat and cook, uncovered, for 25 minutes or until the lentils are soft and the vegetables are tender.

4. Stir in the parsley. Ladle into warmed bowls and serve with toast.

Pasta & Chickpea Soup with Pesto

Preparation Time 25 minutes • Cooking Time about 1 hour • Serves 6 • Per Serving 211 calories,
8g fat (of which 1g saturates), 26g carbohydrate, 0.3g salt • Easy

3 tbsp olive oil
1 onion, chopped
2 garlic cloves, finely chopped
1 small leek, trimmed and sliced
1 tsp freshly chopped rosemary
400g can chickpeas
1,1 litres (2 pints) vegetable stock
4 ripe tomatoes, skinned and
   chopped
1 courgette, diced
125g (4oz) shelled peas

125g (4oz) French beans, halved
125g (4oz) shelled broad beans
50g (2oz) dried pastina (small soup
   pasta)
2 tbsp freshly chopped parsley
salt and ground black pepper
fresh ready-made pesto (see
   Cook's Tip) and freshly grated
   pecorino or Parmesan to serve

1. Heat the oil in a large pan, add the onion, garlic, leek and rosemary and fry gently for 5–6 minutes or until softened but not coloured. Add the chickpeas with their liquid, the stock and tomatoes. Bring to the boil, then reduce the heat, cover the pan and simmer for 40 minutes.

2. Add the courgette, peas, French beans and broad beans. Return to the boil, then reduce the heat and simmer for 10 minutes. Add the pasta and parsley and simmer for 6–8 minutes until al dente. Season to taste with salt and pepper.

3. Ladle into warmed bowls and serve topped with a spoonful of pesto and a sprinkling of cheese.

COOK'S TIP

This broth is also good with a tablespoon of pesto (see below) added to each bowl and served with chunks of crusty bread.
Pesto
Put a 20g pack of roughly chopped basil into a food processor. Add 25g (1oz) finely grated Parmesan, 50g (2oz) pinenuts and 4 tbsp extra virgin olive oil and whiz to a rough paste. Alternatively, grind in a pestle and mortar. Season with salt and plenty of ground black pepper.

Autumn Barley Soup

Preparation Time 10 minutes • Cooking Time 1 hour 5 minutes • Serves 4 • Per Serving 86 calories, trace fat (of which 0.2g saturates), 17g carbohydrate, 0.1g salt • Vegetarian • Dairy Free • Easy

25g (1oz) pot barley, washed
   and drained
1 litre (1¾ pints) vegetable stock
2 large carrots, diced
1 turnip, diced
2 leeks, trimmed and sliced
2 celery sticks, diced
1 small onion, finely chopped
1 bouquet garni (see Cook's Tip)
2 tbsp freshly chopped parsley
salt and ground black pepper

1. Put the barley and stock into a pan and bring to the boil. Reduce the heat and simmer for 45 minutes or until the barley is tender.

2. Add the vegetables to the pan with the bouquet garni and season to taste with black pepper. Bring to the boil, then reduce the heat and simmer for about 20 minutes or until the vegetables are tender.

3. Discard the bouquet garni. Add the parsley to the soup, season to taste with salt and pepper and stir well, then ladle into warmed bowls and serve immediately.

COOK'S TIP
To make a bouquet garni, tie together a sprig each of thyme and parsley with a bay leaf and a piece of celery.

Quick Winter Minestrone

Preparation Time 10 minutes • Cooking Time 45 minutes • Serves 4 • Per Serving 334 calories, 11g fat (of which 3g saturates), 47g carbohydrate, 1.5g salt • Dairy Free • Easy

2 tbsp olive oil
1 small onion, finely chopped
1 carrot, chopped
1 celery stick, chopped
1 garlic clove, crushed
2 tbsp freshly chopped thyme
1 litre (1¾ pints) vegetable stock
400g can chopped tomatoes
400g can borlotti beans, drained
   and rinsed
125g (4oz) minestrone pasta
175g (6oz) Savoy cabbage, shredded
salt and ground black pepper
fresh ready-made pesto (see
   page 16), toasted ciabatta and
   extra virgin olive oil to serve

1. Heat the oil in a large pan and add the onion, carrot and celery. Cook for 8–10 minutes until softened, then add the garlic and thyme. Fry for another 2–3 minutes.

2. Add the stock, tomatoes and half the borlotti beans and bring to the boil. Mash the remaining beans and stir into the soup, then reduce the heat and simmer for 30 minutes, adding the minestrone pasta and cabbage for the last 10 minutes of cooking time.

3. Check the seasoning and correct, if necessary. Ladle into warmed bowls and serve with a dollop of fresh pesto on top and slices of toasted ciabatta drizzled with extra virgin olive oil on the side.

Mulligatawny Soup

Preparation Time 5 minutes • Cooking Time 40 minutes • Serves 4 • Per Serving 252 calories, 13g fat (of which 4g saturates), 7g carbohydrate, 0.9g salt • Easy

3 rashers streaky bacon, rinded and finely chopped
550g (1¼lb) chicken portions
600ml (1 pint) hot chicken stock
1 carrot, sliced
1 celery stick, chopped
1 apple, cored and chopped
2 tsp curry powder
4 peppercorns, crushed
1 clove
1 bay leaf
1 tbsp plain flour
150ml (¼ pint) milk
50g (2oz) long-grain rice, cooked, and crusty bread to serve

1. Fry the bacon in a large pan until the fat begins to run. Do not allow the bacon to become brown.

2. Add the chicken and brown well. Drain the meat on kitchen paper and pour off the fat.

3. Return the bacon and chicken to the pan and add the hot stock and next seven ingredients. Cover the pan and simmer for about 30 minutes or until the chicken is tender.

4. Remove the chicken and allow to cool a little. Cut off the meat and return it to the soup. Discard the clove and bay leaf and reheat the soup gently.

5. Mix the flour with a little cold water. Add to the soup with the milk and reheat without boiling.

6. Ladle the soup into warmed bowls, spoon a mound of rice into each one and serve immediately with crusty bread.

Hearty Chicken Soup with Dumplings

Preparation Time 20 minutes • Cooking Time 40 minutes • Serves 4 • Per Serving 335 calories,
15g fat (of which 5g saturates), 31g carbohydrate, 0.3g salt • Easy

2 tbsp olive oil
2 celery sticks, roughly chopped
150g (5oz) carrots, roughly chopped
150g (5oz) waxy salad potatoes,
    thinly sliced
275g (10oz) chicken breast, thinly
    sliced
2 litres (3½ pints) hot chicken stock
75g (3oz) frozen peas
salt and ground black pepper
a handful of chives, roughly
    chopped, to garnish (optional)

FOR THE DUMPLINGS
100g (3½oz) plain flour
½ tsp baking powder
½ tsp salt
1 medium egg, well beaten
25g (1oz) butter, melted
a splash of milk

1. Heat the oil in a large pan,
then add the celery, carrots and
potatoes. Cook for 5 minutes or until
the vegetables are beginning to
caramelise around the edges. Add
the chicken and fry for 3 minutes or
until just starting to turn golden.
Pour in the hot stock and simmer for
15 minutes, skimming the surface
occasionally to remove any scum.

2. To make the dumplings, sift the
flour, baking powder and salt into
a bowl, then season with black
pepper. Combine the egg, melted
butter and milk in a separate bowl,
then stir quickly into the flour to
make a stiff batter.

3. Drop half-teaspoonfuls of the
dumpling mixture into the soup,
then cover and simmer for a
further 15 minutes.

4. Stir in the peas and heat
through. Check the seasoning,
sprinkle with pepper and serve
garnished with chives, if you like.

Parsnip Soup with Chorizo

Preparation Time 20 minutes • Cooking Time 1 hour • Serves 8 • Per Serving 278 calories, 20g fat (of which 9g saturates), 18g carbohydrate, 0.7g salt • Gluten Free • Easy

40g (1½oz) butter

1 onion, roughly chopped

225g (8oz) floury potatoes, such as
    King Edward, chopped

400g (14oz) parsnips, chopped

4 tsp paprika, plus extra to dust

1.1 litres (2 pints) vegetable stock

450ml (¾ pint) milk

4 tbsp double cream

75g (3oz) sliced chorizo sausage,
    cut into fine strips

salt and ground black pepper

parsnip crisps and freshly grated
    Parmesan to serve

1. Melt the butter in a large heavy-based pan over a gentle heat. Add the onion and cook for 5 minutes or until soft. Add the potatoes, parsnips and paprika. Mix well and cook gently, stirring occasionally, for 15 minutes or until the vegetables begin to soften.

2. Add the stock, milk and cream and season with salt and pepper. Bring to the boil, then reduce the heat and simmer for about 25 minutes or until the vegetables are very soft. Add 50g (2oz) of the chorizo. Allow the soup to cool a little, then whiz in a blender or food processor until smooth. The soup can be thinned with additional stock or milk, if you like. Check the seasoning and put back in the pan.

3. To serve, reheat the soup. Serve in warmed bowls and top each with parsnip crisps. Sprinkle with the remaining chorizo and a little Parmesan, and dust with paprika.

FREEZING TIP

To freeze Complete the recipe to the end of step 2, then cool, pack and freeze for up to one month.
To use Thaw the soup overnight at cool room temperature, then complete the recipe.

Turkey & Chestnut Soup

Preparation Time 5 minutes • Cooking Time 45 minutes • Serves 4 • Per Serving 330 calories,
10g fat (of which 5g saturates), 52g carbohydrate, 0.2g salt • Gluten Free • Easy

25g (1oz) butter or margarine
1 large onion, chopped
225g (8oz) Brussels sprouts
900ml (1½ pints) turkey stock
   made from leftover carcass and
   any leftover turkey meat
400g can whole chestnuts, drained
2 tsp freshly chopped thyme or
   1 tsp dried thyme
salt and ground black pepper
stock or milk to finish
thyme sprigs to garnish

1. Melt the fat in a large heavy-based pan, add the onion and fry gently for 5 minutes or until it has softened.

2. Trim the sprouts and cut a cross in the base of each one. Add to the onion, cover the pan with a lid and cook gently for 5 minutes, shaking the pan frequently.

3. Pour in the stock and bring to the boil, then add the remaining ingredients, with salt and pepper to taste. Reduce the heat, cover the pan and simmer for 30 minutes or until the vegetables are tender.

4. Leave the soup to cool a little, then whiz in batches in a blender or food processor until smooth. Return to the rinsed-out pan and reheat gently, then thin down with either stock or milk, according to taste.

5. Taste and adjust the seasoning. To serve, ladle into warmed bowls and garnish with sprigs of thyme.

COOK'S TIP
Serve for an informal family lunch with hot garlic bread, wholemeal toast, cheese on toast or hot sausage rolls.

Hot & Sour Soup

Preparation Time 20 minutes • Cooking Time 30–35 minutes • Serves 4 • Per Serving 255 calories, 10g fat (of which 1g saturates), 19g carbohydrate, 0.7g salt • Dairy Free • Easy

1 tbsp vegetable oil

2 turkey breasts, about 300g (11oz), or the same quantity of tofu, cut into strips

5cm (2in) piece fresh root ginger, peeled and grated

4 spring onions, finely sliced

1–2 tbsp Thai red curry paste

75g (3oz) long-grain wild rice

1.1 litres (2 pints) hot weak chicken or vegetable stock or boiling water

200g (7oz) mangetouts, sliced

juice of 1 lime

4 tbsp roughly chopped fresh coriander to garnish

1. Heat the oil in a deep pan. Add the turkey or tofu and cook over a medium heat for 5 minutes or until browned. Add the ginger and spring onions and cook for a further 2–3 minutes. Stir in the curry paste and cook for 1–2 minutes to warm the spices.

2. Add the rice and stir to coat in the curry paste. Pour the hot stock or boiling water into the pan, stir once and bring to the boil. Reduce the heat, cover the pan and simmer for 20 minutes.

3. Add the mangetouts and cook for a further 5 minutes or until the rice is cooked. Just before serving, squeeze in the lime juice and stir to mix.

4. To serve, ladle into warmed bowls and sprinkle with the coriander.

Spicy Lamb Soup

Preparation Time 15 minutes • Cooking Time about 1 hour • Serves 4 • Per serving 367 calories, 17g fat (of which 6g saturates), 31g carbohydrate, 0.6g salt • Gluten Free • Dairy Free • Easy

1 tbsp olive oil
350g (12oz) lamb mince
1 medium onion, finely chopped
227g can tomatoes
3 tsp harissa paste
1.5 litres (2½ pints) hot lamb stock
100g (3½oz) couscous
410g can chickpeas, drained
    and rinsed
salt and ground black pepper
1 tbsp each freshly chopped
    flat-leafed parsley and mint
    to garnish
flatbread and lemon wedges
    (optional) to serve

1. Heat half the oil in a large pan and brown the mince in batches. Set aside.

2. Add the remaining oil and gently fry the onion for 10 minutes or until softened. Add the tomatoes and harissa and simmer, covered, for 30 minutes.

3. Add the hot stock and couscous and simmer for 10 minutes. Stir in the chickpeas and heat through for 2–3 minutes. Add the herbs and check the seasoning. Serve immediately with warmed flatbread, and lemon wedges, if you like, to squeeze into the soup.

GET AHEAD

To prepare ahead Complete the recipe to the end of step 1. Cool, cover and chill for up to three days. *To use* Complete the recipe.

FISH &
SHELLFISH

Salmon Kedgeree

Preparation Time 15 minutes, plus soaking • Cooking Time 55 minutes • Serves 4 • Per Serving 490 calories, 15g fat (of which 2g saturates), 62g carbohydrate, 0.1g salt • Gluten Free • Easy

50g (2oz) butter
700g (1½lb) onions, sliced
2 tsp garam masala
1 garlic clove, crushed
75g (3oz) split green lentils, soaked in 300ml (½ pint) boiling water for 15 minutes, then drained
750ml (1¼ pints) hot vegetable stock
225g (8oz) basmati rice
1 green chilli, seeded and finely chopped (see page 30)
350g (12oz) salmon fillet
salt and ground black pepper

1. Melt the butter in a flameproof casserole over a medium heat. Add the onions and cook for 5 minutes or until soft. Remove a third of the onions and put to one side. Increase the heat and cook the remaining onions for 10 minutes to caramelise. Remove and put to one side.

2. Put the first batch of onions back into the casserole, add the garam masala and garlic and cook, stirring, for 1 minute. Add the drained lentils and hot stock, cover the pan and cook for 15 minutes. Add the rice and chilli and season with salt and pepper. Bring to the boil, then reduce the heat, cover the pan and simmer for 5 minutes.

3. Put the salmon fillet on top of the rice, cover and continue to cook gently for 15 minutes or until the rice is cooked, the stock absorbed and the salmon opaque.

4. Lift off the salmon and divide into flakes. Put it back into the casserole and fork through the rice. Garnish with the reserved caramelised onion and serve.

COOK'S TIP

Chillies vary enormously in strength, from quite mild to blisteringly hot, depending on the type of chilli and its ripeness. Taste a small piece first to check that it's not too hot for you. When handling chillies, be extremely careful not to touch or rub your eyes with your fingers, as it will make them sting. Wash knives immediately after chopping chillies. As a precaution, use rubber gloves when preparing them if you like.

Spicy Monkfish Stew

Preparation Time 10 minutes • Cooking Time 35 minutes • Serves 6 • Per Serving 142 calories,
3g fat (of which 1g saturates), 16g carbohydrate, 0.2g salt • Dairy Free • Easy

1 tbsp olive oil
1 onion, finely sliced
1 tbsp tom yum paste (see Cook's Tip)
450g (1lb) potatoes, cut into 2cm (¾in) chunks
400g can chopped tomatoes in rich tomato juice
600ml (1 pint) hot fish stock
450g (1lb) monkfish, cut into 2cm (¾in) chunks
200g (7oz) ready-to-eat baby spinach
salt and ground black pepper

1. Heat the oil in a pan over a medium heat and fry the onion for 5 minutes until golden.

2. Add the tom yum paste and potatoes and stir-fry for 1 minute. Add the tomatoes and hot stock, season well with salt and pepper and cover. Bring to the boil, then reduce the heat and simmer, partially covered, for 15 minutes or until the potatoes are just tender.

3. Add the monkfish to the pan and continue to simmer for 5–10 minutes until the fish is cooked. Add the baby spinach leaves and stir through until wilted.

4. Spoon the fish stew into warmed bowls and serve immediately.

COOK'S TIP
Tom yum paste is a hot and spicy Thai mixture used in soups and stews. It is available from large supermarkets and Asian food shops.

Spanish Fish Stew

Preparation Time 20 minutes • Cooking Time 1 hour 10 minutes • Serves 4 • Per Serving 463 calories, 22g fat (of which 6g saturates), 32g carbohydrate, 1.8g salt • Gluten Free • Dairy Free • Easy

t350g (12oz) small salad potatoes, halved
175g (6oz) chorizo sausage, skinned and roughly chopped
350g jar roasted peppers in olive oil, drained and chopped, oil reserved
1 garlic clove, crushed
2 small red onions, cut into thick wedges
175ml (6fl oz) dry white wine
300g (11oz) passata
25g (1oz) pitted black olives
450g (1lb) chunky white fish, such as cod and haddock, cut into large cubes
salt and ground black pepper
freshly chopped flat-leafed parsley to garnish

1. Preheat the oven to 170°C (150°C fan oven) mark 3. Put the potatoes, chorizo, roasted peppers, garlic, onions, wine and passata into a large flameproof casserole with 2 tbsp of the oil from the peppers. Season with salt and pepper.

2. Bring to the boil over a medium heat, then cover with a tight-fitting lid and cook in the oven for 45 minutes.

3. Add the olives and fish and put back in the oven for 15 minutes or until the fish is opaque and completely cooked through. Spoon into warmed bowls and serve garnished with chopped parsley.

COOK'S TIP

Passata is a useful storecupboard ingredient from the Italian kitchen, which can be used in sauces and stews. It is made from ripe tomatoes that have been puréed and sieved to make a very smooth sauce.

Smoked Haddock & Potato Pie

Preparation Time 15 minutes • Cooking Time 1¼ hours–1 hour 25 minutes • Serves 4 • Per Serving 380 calories, 20g fat (of which 11g saturates), 37g carbohydrate, 1.5g salt • Gluten Free • Easy

142ml carton double cream
150ml (¼ pint) fish stock
3 medium baking potatoes, thinly sliced
300g (11oz) skinless smoked haddock fillets, roughly chopped
20g pack fresh chives, chopped
1 large onion, finely chopped
salt and ground black pepper
lemon slice to garnish
green salad to serve

1. Preheat the oven to 200°C (180°C fan oven) mark 6. Pour the cream into a large bowl. Add the fish stock and stir well to combine.

2. Add the potatoes, haddock, chives and onion and season with salt and pepper. Toss everything together to coat. Spoon the mixture into a shallow 2.4 litre (4¼ pint) ovenproof dish.

3. Cover the dish with foil, put it on a baking tray and cook for 45 minutes. Remove the foil and cook for 30–40 minutes until bubbling and the top is golden.

4. To check that the potatoes are cooked, insert a skewer or small knife – it should push in easily. If you like, you can put the dish under a hot grill to make the top layer crisp. Leave to cool slightly, then serve with a green salad.

COOK'S TIP
For the lightest texture, make sure you use floury baking potatoes, as salad potatoes are too waxy.

Baked Salmon with Jersey Royals & Watercress Mayonnaise

Preparation Time 15 minutes • Cooking Time 50 minutes • Serves 6 • Per Serving 560 calories, 41g fat (of which 7g saturates), 15g carbohydrate, 0.8g salt • Gluten Free • Easy

1 tsp fennel seeds (optional)
1 tsp rock salt
2 tbsp olive oil
450g (1lb) Jersey Royal potatoes, sliced thickly
6 skinless salmon fillets
6 slices prosciutto
150g (5oz) good-quality mayonnaise
75g (3oz) plain yogurt
juice of ½ lemon
40g (1½oz) watercress, finely chopped
1 tbsp capers, roughly chopped
300g (11oz) cherry tomatoes on the vine, cut into bunches
salt and ground black pepper
lemon wedges to serve

1. Preheat the oven to 200°C (180°C fan oven) mark 6. Crush the fennel seeds, if using, and the salt in a pestle and mortar. Put into a bowl with half the oil, then add the potatoes and toss. Layer the potatoes in a large roasting dish and cover with foil. Cook in the oven for 20 minutes.

2. Check the fish for stray bones, then season with salt and pepper. Wrap a slice of prosciutto around the middle of each fillet, making sure the seam is underneath.

3. Mix the mayonnaise with the yogurt and lemon juice. Stir in the watercress and capers and check the seasoning.

4. Remove the foil from the potatoes and continue cooking for 10 minutes or until they are almost tender. Arrange the tomatoes and fish on top of the potatoes, then sprinkle the fish with the remaining oil. Cook for 15–20 minutes.

5. Serve with the lemon mayonnaise and lemon wedges.

POULTRY & GAME

One-pot Chicken

Preparation Time 20 minutes • Cooking Time 1 hour 40 minutes • Serves 6 • Per Serving 474 calories, 33g fat (of which 9g saturates), 6g carbohydrate, 0.6g salt • Dairy Free • Easy

2 tbsp olive oil

1 large onion, cut into wedges

2 rindless streaky bacon rashers, chopped

1 chicken, about 1.6kg (3½lb)

6 carrots

2 small turnips, cut into wedges

1 garlic clove, crushed

bouquet garni (1 bay leaf, a few fresh parsley and thyme sprigs)

600ml (1 pint) hot chicken stock

100ml (3½fl oz) dry white wine

12 button mushrooms

3 tbsp freshly chopped flat-leafed parsley

salt and ground black pepper

mashed potatoes to serve (optional)

1. Heat the oil in a non-stick flameproof casserole, then add the onion and bacon and fry for 5 minutes or until golden. Remove and set aside.

2. Add the whole chicken to the casserole and fry for 10 minutes, turning carefully to brown all over. Remove and set aside.

3. Preheat the oven to 200°C (180°C fan oven) mark 6. Add the carrots, turnips and garlic to the casserole. Fry for 5 minutes, then add the bacon and onion. Put the chicken back into the casserole, add the bouquet garni, hot stock and wine and season with salt and pepper. Bring to a simmer, then cover the pan and cook in the oven for 30 minutes.

4. Remove the casserole from the oven and add the mushrooms. Baste the chicken, then re-cover and cook for a further 50 minutes.

5. Lift out the chicken, then stir the parsley into the cooking liquid. Carve the chicken and serve with the vegetables and cooking liquid, and mashed potatoes, if you like.

TRY SOMETHING DIFFERENT

Use chicken pieces such as drumsticks or thighs, reducing the cooking time in step 4 to 20 minutes.

Slow-braised Garlic Chicken

Preparation Time 30 minutes, plus cooling • Cooking time about 2 hours • Serves 6 •
Per Serving 506 calories, 28g fat (of which 9g saturates), 10g carbohydrate, 1g salt • Easy

2 tbsp olive oil

1 tbsp freshly chopped thyme

**125g (4oz) chestnut mushrooms,
    finely chopped**

**6 whole chicken legs (drumsticks
    and thighs)**

18 thin slices pancetta

2 tbsp plain flour

25g (1oz) butter

18 small shallots

12 garlic cloves, unpeeled but split

**750ml bottle full-bodied white
    wine, such as Chardonnay**

2 bay leaves

**salt and freshly ground black
    pepper**

1. Preheat the oven to 180°C (160°C fan oven) mark 4. Heat 1 tbsp of the oil in a frying pan. Add the thyme and mushrooms and fry until the moisture has evaporated. Season with salt and ground black pepper and leave to cool.

2. Loosen the skin away from one chicken leg and spoon a little of the mushroom paste underneath. Season the leg all over with salt and pepper, then wrap three pancetta slices around the thigh end. Repeat with the remaining chicken legs, then dust using 1 tbsp of the flour.

3. Melt the butter in a frying pan with the remaining oil over a high heat. Fry the chicken legs, in batches, seam side down, until golden. Turn the legs and brown the other side – the browning should take 8–10 minutes per batch, then transfer to a casserole.

4. Put the shallots and garlic into the frying pan and cook for 10 minutes or until browned. Sprinkle with the remaining flour and cook for 1 minute. Pour in the wine and bring to the boil, stirring. Pour into the casserole with the chicken and add the bay leaves. Cover and cook in the oven for 1½ hours. Serve hot.

FREEZE AHEAD

To make ahead and freeze, complete the recipe. Cool quickly, then freeze in an airtight container for up to one month. To use, thaw overnight at cool room temperature. Preheat the oven to 220°C (200°C fan oven) mark 7. Put the chicken back into the casserole and reheat in the oven for 15 minutes. Reduce the oven temperature to 180°C (160°C fan oven) mark 4 and cook for a further 25 minutes.

Stoved Chicken

Preparation Time 15 minutes • Cooking Time about 2½ hours • Serves 4 •
Per Serving 854 calories, 45g fat (of which 14g saturates), 55g carbohydrate, 3g salt • Easy

25g (1oz) butter, plus a little extra
1 tbsp vegetable oil
4 chicken quarters, halved
**125g (4oz) lean back bacon, rind
    removed and chopped**
**1.1kg (2½lb) floury potatoes, such
    as King Edward, cut into 5mm
    (¼in) slices**

2 large onions, sliced
**2 tsp freshly chopped thyme or
    ½ tsp dried thyme**
600ml (1 pint) hot chicken stock
**salt and freshly ground black
    pepper**
snipped fresh chives to garnish

1. Preheat the oven to 150°C
(130°C fan oven) mark 2. Heat
half the butter and the oil in a large
frying pan and fry the chicken
and bacon for 5 minutes or until
lightly browned.

2. Layer half the potato slices, then
half the onion slices in the bottom
of a large casserole. Season well,
add the thyme and dot with half the
remaining butter.

3. Add the chicken and bacon,
season to taste and dot with
the remaining butter. Cover
with the remaining onions and
finally a layer of potatoes. Season
and dot with a little more butter.
Pour the hot stock over.

4. Cover and cook in the oven for
about 2½ hours until the chicken
is tender and the potatoes are
cooked, adding a little more hot
stock if necessary.

5. Just before serving, sprinkle
with snipped chives.

Classic Coq au Vin

Preparation Time 15 minutes • Cooking Time about 2¼ hours • Serves 6 • Per Serving 740 calories, 44g fat (of which 17g saturates), 26g carbohydrate, 1.8g salt • Easy

1 large chicken, jointed (see page 228), or 6–8 chicken joints
2 tbsp well-seasoned flour
100g (3½oz) butter
125g (4oz) lean bacon, diced
1 medium onion, quartered
1 medium carrot, quartered
4 tbsp brandy
600ml (1 pint) red wine
1 garlic clove, crushed
1 bouquet garni (2 bay leaves, a few fresh parsley and thyme sprigs)
1 tsp sugar
2 tbsp vegetable oil
450g (1lb) button onions
a pinch of sugar
1 tsp wine vinegar
225g (8oz) button mushrooms
6 slices white bread, crusts removed
salt and freshly ground black pepper

1. Coat the chicken pieces with 1 tbsp of the seasoned flour. Melt 25g (1oz) of the butter in a flameproof casserole. Add the chicken and fry until golden brown on all sides. Add the bacon, onion quarters and carrot and fry until softened.

2. Heat the brandy in a small pan, pour over the chicken and ignite, shaking the pan. Pour in the wine and stir to dislodge any sediment from the bottom of the casserole. Add the garlic, bouquet garni and sugar cube and bring to the boil. Reduce the heat, cover and simmer for 1–1½ hours until the chicken is cooked through.

3. Meanwhile, melt 25g (1oz) of the butter with 1 tsp of the oil in a frying pan. Add the button onions and fry until they begin to brown. Add the sugar and vinegar together with 1 tbsp water. Cover and simmer for 10–15 minutes until just tender. Keep warm.

4. Melt 25g (1oz) of the butter with 2 tsp of the oil in a pan. Add the mushrooms and cook for a few minutes, then turn off the heat and keep warm. Remove the chicken from the casserole and place in a dish. Surround with the onions and mushrooms and keep hot.

5. Discard the bouquet garni. Skim the excess fat from the cooking liquid, then boil for 3–5 minutes until reduced. Add the remaining oil to the fat in the frying pan and fry the bread until golden brown on both sides. Cut each slice into triangles.

6. Work the remaining butter and flour together to make a beurre manié. Take the casserole off the heat and add small pieces of the beurre manié to the liquid. Stir until smooth, then put back on the hob and bring just to the boil. The sauce should be thick and shiny. Take off the heat and season. Put the chicken, onions and mushrooms back into the casserole and stir. Serve with the fried bread.

Chicken Cacciatore

Preparation Time 5 minutes • Cooking Time 40 minutes • Serves 4 • Per Serving 327 calories,
17g fat (of which 4g saturates), 3g carbohydrate, 1.3g salt • Gluten Free • Dairy Free • Easy

2 tbsp olive oil
8 boneless, skinless chicken thighs
2 garlic cloves, crushed
1 tsp dried thyme
1 tsp dried tarragon
150ml (¼ pint) white wine
400g can chopped tomatoes
12 pitted black olives
12 capers, rinsed and drained
ground black pepper
brown rice and broad beans or peas
  to serve

1. Heat the oil in a flameproof casserole over a high heat. Add the chicken and brown all over. Reduce the heat and add the garlic, thyme, tarragon and wine to the casserole. Stir for 1 minute, then add the tomatoes and season with pepper.

2. Bring to the boil, then reduce the heat, cover the casserole and simmer for 20 minutes or until the chicken is tender.

3. Lift the chicken out of the casserole and put to one side. Bubble the sauce for 5 minutes or until thickened, add the olives and capers, stir well and cook for a further 2–3 minutes.

4. Put the chicken into the sauce. Serve with brown rice and broad beans or peas.

Alsace Chicken

Preparation Time 20 minutes • Cooking Time 1 hour 20 minutes • Serves 4 • Per Serving 484 calories, 24g fat (of which 8g saturates), 11g carbohydrate, 1.4g salt • Easy

2 tbsp vegetable oil

8 chicken pieces (such as breasts, thighs and drumsticks)

125g (4oz) rindless smoked streaky bacon rashers, cut into strips

12 shallots, peeled but left whole

3 fresh tarragon sprigs

1 tbsp plain flour

150ml (¼ pint) Alsace Riesling white wine

500ml (18fl oz) hot chicken stock

3 tbsp crème fraîche

salt and ground black pepper

new potatoes (optional) and green vegetables to serve

1. Heat half the oil in a frying pan over a medium heat. Fry the chicken, in batches, until golden, adding more oil to the pan as necessary. Set aside.

2. Put the bacon into the same pan and fry gently to release its fat. Add the shallots and cook for 5 minutes, stirring occasionally, or until both the shallots and bacon are lightly coloured.

3. Strip the leaves from the tarragon and set both the leaves and stalks aside. Sprinkle the flour over the shallots and bacon and stir to absorb the juices. Cook for 1 minute, then gradually add the wine, hot stock and tarragon stalks. Put the chicken back into the pan, cover and simmer over a gentle heat for 45 minutes–1 hour until the chicken is cooked through.

4. Remove the chicken, bacon and shallots with a slotted spoon and keep warm. Discard the tarragon stalks. Bubble the sauce until reduced by half. Stir in the crème fraîche and tarragon leaves. Season with salt and pepper.

5. Turn off the heat, put the chicken, bacon and shallots back into the pan and stir to combine. Serve with new potatoes, if you like, and green vegetables.

Chicken with Green Olives & Lemons

Preparation Time 15 minutes • Cooking Time about 1 hour 20 minutes • Serves 6 • Per Serving 347 calories, 22g fat (of which 5g saturates), 7g carbohydrate, 0.9g salt • Dairy Free • Easy

½ tsp each ground turmeric,
  ginger and coriander
1½ tbsp plain flour
6 chicken legs, with skin on
2 tbsp olive oil
1 medium onion, roughly chopped
1 garlic clove, thinly sliced
100ml (3½fl oz) manzanilla or fino
  sherry
900ml (1½ pints) hot chicken stock
3 preserved lemons
75g (3oz) green olives, sliced
juice of ½ lemon
salt and ground black pepper

1. Put the spices and flour into a polythene bag and season. Add the chicken and shake until covered with the flour mixture. Shake off the excess and set aside any leftover flour.

2. Heat 1 tbsp oil in a large flameproof casserole over a medium heat. Fry the chicken in batches until golden. Avoid overcrowding the pan, as it will lower the temperature and the chicken won't brown. Remove the chicken and set aside.

3. Put the remaining oil into the same pan and cook the onion over a low heat for 10 minutes. Add the garlic and cook for 1 minute. Turn up the heat to medium and add the leftover flour. Cook for 1 minute, stirring to soak up the oil. Scrape up any browned bits from the base of the pan – these will add flavour. Gradually stir in the sherry (it will bubble and thicken), followed by the hot stock.

4. Halve the lemons, scrape out the pulp and discard. Add the peel to the pan along with the chicken. Cover the pan and simmer over a low heat for 30 minutes. Stir in the olives and cook for 15 minutes or until the chicken is done – the juices should run clear when you pierce the flesh with a knife.

5. Remove the chicken, olives, onions and lemons with a slotted spoon (don't worry if you leave some onion behind) and keep them warm. Turn up the heat and boil the sauce rapidly until it reduces by about one-third and turns syrupy. Taste and add more seasoning if it needs it, along with the lemon juice.

6. Return the chicken, olives, onion and lemons to the casserole and serve from the dish.

COOK'S TIP

If you have leftover preserved lemons, the next time you roast a whole chicken pop a couple inside the bird along with a few thyme sprigs.

Chicken with Fennel & Tarragon

Preparation Time 10 minutes • Cooking Time 45–55 minutes • Serves 4 • Per Serving 334 calories, 26g fat (of which 15g saturates), 3g carbohydrate, 0.5g salt • Gluten Free • Easy

1 tbsp olive oil
4 chicken thighs
1 onion, finely chopped
1 fennel bulb, sliced
juice of ½ lemon
200ml (7fl oz) hot chicken stock
200g (7oz) half-fat crème fraîche
1 small bunch of tarragon, roughly
   chopped
wild rice to serve

1. Preheat the oven to 200°C (180°C fan oven) mark 6. Heat the oil in a large flameproof casserole. Add the chicken thighs and fry for 5 minutes or until brown, then remove and set them aside to keep warm.

2. Add the onion to the pan and fry for 5 minutes, then add the fennel and cook for 5–10 minutes until softened.

3. Add the lemon juice to the pan, then add the hot stock. Bring to a simmer and cook until the liquid is reduced by half.

4. Stir in the crème fraîche and return the chicken to the pan. Stir once to mix, then cover and cook in the oven for 25–30 minutes. Stir the tarragon into the sauce and serve with wild rice.

Chicken & Coconut Curry

Preparation Time 15 minutes • Cooking Time 35 minutes • Serves 6 • Per Serving 204 calories,
6g fat (of which 1g saturates), 10g carbohydrate, 1.5g salt • Gluten Free • Dairy Free • Easy

2 garlic cloves, peeled
1 onion, quartered
1 lemongrass stalk, trimmed and
   halved
2.5cm (1in) piece fresh root ginger,
   peeled and halved
2 small hot chillies (see page 30)
a small handful of fresh coriander
1 tsp ground coriander
grated zest and juice of 1 lime
2 tbsp vegetable oil

6 boneless, skinless chicken
   breasts, each cut into three
   pieces
2 large tomatoes, skinned and
   chopped
2 tbsp Thai fish sauce
900ml (1½ pints) coconut milk
salt and ground black pepper
finely sliced red chilli to garnish
basmati rice to serve

1. Put the garlic, onion, lemongrass, ginger, chillies, fresh coriander, ground coriander and lime zest and juice into a food processor and whiz to a paste. Add a little water if the mixture gets stuck under the blades.

2. Heat the oil in a wok or large frying pan, add the spice paste and cook over a fairly high heat for 3–4 minutes, stirring constantly. Add the chicken and cook for 5 minutes, stirring to coat in the spice mixture.

3. Add the tomatoes, fish sauce and coconut milk. Simmer, covered, for about 25 minutes or until the chicken is cooked. Season with salt and pepper, garnish with red chilli and serve with basmati rice.

Chicken & Vegetable Hotpot

Preparation Time 5 minutes • Cooking Time 30 minutes • Serves 4 • Per Serving 338 calories,
14g fat (of which 3g saturates), 14g carbohydrate, 1.2g salt • Dairy Free • Easy

**4 chicken breasts, with skin on,
about 125g (4oz) each
2 large parsnips, chopped
2 large carrots, chopped
300ml (½ pint) ready-made gravy
125g (4oz) cabbage, shredded
ground black pepper**

1. Heat a non-stick frying pan or flameproof casserole until hot. Add the chicken breasts, skin side down, and cook for 5–6 minutes. Turn them over, add the parsnips and carrots and cook for a further 7–8 minutes.

2. Pour the gravy over the chicken and vegetables, then cover the pan and cook gently for 10 minutes.

3. Season with pepper and stir in the cabbage, then cover and continue to cook for 4–5 minutes until the chicken is cooked through, the cabbage has wilted and the vegetables are tender. Serve hot.

Oven-baked Chicken with Garlic Potatoes

Preparation Time 10 minutes • Cooking Time 1½ hours • Serves 6 • Per Serving 376 calories, 16g fat (of which 5g saturates), 32g carbohydrate, 1.2g salt • Easy

- 2 medium baking potatoes, thinly sliced
- a little freshly grated nutmeg
- 600ml (1 pint) white sauce (use a ready-made sauce or make your own, see Cook's Tip)
- ½ × 390g can fried onions
- 250g (9oz) frozen peas
- 450g (1lb) cooked chicken, shredded
- 20g pack garlic butter, sliced
- a little butter to grease
- salt and ground black pepper
- granary bread to serve (optional)

1. Preheat the oven to 180°C (160°C fan oven) mark 4. Layer half the potatoes over the base of a 2.4 litre (4¼ pint) shallow ovenproof dish and season with the nutmeg, salt and pepper. Pour the white sauce over and shake the dish, so that the sauce settles through the gaps in the potatoes.

2. Spread half the onions on top, then scatter on half the peas. Arrange the shredded chicken on top, then add the remaining peas and onions. Finish with the remaining potatoes, arranged in an even layer, and dot with garlic butter. Season with salt and pepper.

3. Cover tightly with buttered foil and cook for 1 hour. Turn up the heat to 200°C (180°C fan oven) mark 6, remove the foil and continue to cook for 20–30 minutes until the potatoes are golden and tender. Serve with granary bread, if you like, to mop up the juices.

COOK'S TIP

White Sauce

To make 600ml (1 pint) white sauce, melt 25g (1oz) butter in a pan, then stir in 25g (1oz) plain flour. Cook, stirring constantly, for 1 minute. Remove from the heat and gradually pour in 600ml (1 pint) milk, beating after each addition. Return to the heat and cook, stirring, until the sauce has thickened and is velvety and smooth. Season with salt, black pepper and freshly grated nutmeg.

Herb Chicken with Roasted Vegetables

Preparation Time 15 minutes, plus marinating • Cooking Time 40 minutes • Serves 4 • Per Serving 453 calories, 29g fat (of which 7g saturates), 10g carbohydrate, 0.3g salt • Gluten Free • Dairy Free • Easy

2 garlic cloves
25g (1oz) fresh basil
25g (1oz) fresh mint
8 fresh lemon thyme sprigs
4 tbsp olive oil
4 whole chicken legs (drumsticks and thighs)
1 small aubergine, chopped
200g (7oz) baby plum tomatoes
2 red peppers, seeded and chopped
2 courgettes, sliced
juice of 1 lemon
salt and ground black pepper
green salad to serve

1. Put the garlic, two-thirds of the basil and mint and the leaves from 4 lemon thyme sprigs into a food processor and whiz, adding half the oil gradually until the mixture forms a thick paste. (Alternatively, use a mortar and pestle.)

2. Rub the paste over the chicken legs, then put into a bowl. Cover, then chill and leave to marinate for at least 30 minutes.

3. Preheat the oven to 200°C (180°C fan oven) mark 6. Put the aubergine, plum tomatoes, red peppers and courgettes into a large roasting tin with the remaining oil and season with salt and pepper. Toss to coat. Add the chicken and roast for 30–40 minutes until the vegetables are tender and the chicken cooked through.

4. Squeeze the lemon juice over and stir in the remaining herbs. Serve immediately with a crisp green salad.

Jambalaya

Preparation Time 15 minutes • Cooking Time about 50 minutes, plus standing • Serves 4 • Per Serving 558 calories,
25g fat (of which 6g saturates), 49g carbohydrate, 0g salt • Gluten Free • Dairy Free • Easy

2 tbsp olive oil
300g (11oz) boneless, skinless
   chicken thighs, cut into chunks
75g (3oz) French sausage, such as
   saucisse sèche, chopped
2 celery sticks, chopped
1 large onion, finely chopped
225g (8oz) long-grain rice
1 tbsp tomato purée
2 tsp Cajun spice mix
500ml (18fl oz) hot chicken stock
1 bay leaf
4 large tomatoes, roughly chopped
200g (7oz) raw tiger prawns, peeled
   and deveined (see Cook's Tip)

1. Heat 1 tbsp oil in a large pan and fry the chicken and sausage over a medium heat until browned. Remove with a slotted spoon and set aside.

2. Add the remaining oil to the pan with the celery and onion. Fry gently for 15 minutes or until the vegetables are softened but not coloured. Tip in the rice and stir for 1 minute to coat in the oil. Add the tomato purée and spice mix and cook for another 2 minutes.

3. Pour in the hot stock and return the browned chicken and sausage to the pan with the bay leaf and tomatoes. Simmer for 20–25 minutes until the stock has been fully absorbed and the rice is cooked.

4. Stir in the prawns and cover the pan. Leave to stand for 10 minutes or until the prawns have turned pink. Serve immediately.

COOK'S TIPS

To devein prawns, pull off the head and discard (or put to one side and use later for making stock). Using pointed scissors, cut through the soft shell on the belly side. Prise off the shell, leaving the tail attached. (The shell can also be used later for making stock.) Using a small sharp knife, make a shallow cut along the back of the prawn. Using the point of the knife, remove and discard the black vein (the intestinal tract) that runs along the back of the prawn.

Classic Paella

Preparation Time 15 minutes, plus infusing • Cooking Time 50 minutes • Serves 6 • Per Serving 554 calories, 16g fat (of which 3g saturates), 58g carbohydrate, 0.5g salt • Dairy Free • A Little Effort

1 litre (1¾ pints) chicken stock
½ tsp saffron threads
6 boneless, skinless chicken thighs
5 tbsp extra virgin olive oil
1 large onion, chopped
4 large garlic cloves, crushed
1 tsp paprika
2 red peppers, seeded and sliced
400g can chopped tomatoes
350g (12oz) long-grain rice
200ml (7fl oz) dry sherry
500g (1lb 2oz) cooked mussels
200g (7oz) cooked tiger prawns
juice of ½ lemon
salt and ground black pepper
lemon wedges and fresh flat-leafed
    parsley to serve

1. Heat the stock, then add the saffron and leave to infuse for 30 minutes. Meanwhile, cut each chicken thigh into three pieces.

2. Heat half the oil in a large frying pan and, working in batches, fry the chicken for 3–5 minutes until pale golden brown. Set the chicken aside.

3. Reduce the heat slightly and add the remaining oil. Fry the onion for 5 minutes or until soft. Add the garlic and paprika and stir for 1 minute. Add the chicken, red peppers and tomatoes.

4. Stir in the rice, then add one-third of the stock and bring to the boil. Season with salt and pepper.

5. Reduce the heat to a simmer. Cook, uncovered, stirring continuously, until most of the liquid is absorbed.

6. Add the remaining stock a little at a time, letting it become absorbed into the rice before adding more – this should take about 25 minutes. Add the sherry and continue cooking for another 2 minutes – the rice should be quite wet, as it will continue to absorb liquid.

7. Add the mussels and prawns to the pan, including all their juices, with the lemon juice. Stir them in and cook for 5 minutes to heat through. Adjust the seasoning, then garnish with lemon wedges and fresh parsley and serve.

Spiced Chicken Pilau

Preparation Time 15 minutes • Cooking Time 35–40 minutes • Serves 4 • Per Serving 649 calories,
18g fat (of which 2g saturates), 87g carbohydrate, 2.8g salt • Dairy Free • Easy

50g (2oz) pinenuts

2 tbsp olive oil

2 onions, sliced

2 garlic cloves, crushed

2 tbsp medium curry powder

6 boneless, skinless chicken thighs
or 450g (1lb) skinless cooked
chicken, cut into strips

350g (12oz) American easy-cook
rice

2 tsp salt

a pinch of saffron threads

50g (2oz) sultanas

225g (8oz) ripe tomatoes, roughly
chopped

1. Spread the pinenuts over a
baking sheet and toast under
a hot grill until golden brown,
turning them frequently. Put to
one side.

2. Heat the oil in a large heavy-
based pan over a medium heat.
Add the onions and garlic and
cook for 5 minutes or until soft.
Remove half the onion mixture
and put to one side.

3. Add the curry powder and
cook for 1 minute, then add the
chicken and stir. Cook for another
10 minutes if the meat is raw, or
for 4 minutes if you're using
cooked chicken, stirring from
time to time until browned.

4. Add the rice to the pan and
stir to coat in the oil, then add
900ml (1½ pints) boiling water,
the salt and saffron. Cover the
pan and bring to the boil, then
reduce the heat to low and cook
for 20 minutes or until the rice is
tender and most of the liquid has
been absorbed. Stir in the reserved
onion mixture and the sultanas,
tomatoes and pinenuts. Cook for a
further 5 minutes to warm through,
then serve.

COOK'S TIP
*This is a good way to use leftover
roast turkey.*

Moroccan Chicken with Chickpeas

Preparation Time 10 minutes • Cooking Time 50 minutes • Serves 6 • Per Serving 440 calories, 18g fat (of which 6g saturates), 33g carbohydrate, 1g salt • Easy

12 chicken pieces, including thighs, drumsticks and breasts
25g (1oz) butter
1 large onion, sliced
2 garlic cloves, crushed
2 tbsp harissa paste
a generous pinch of saffron threads
1 tsp salt
1 cinnamon stick
600ml (1 pint) chicken stock
75g (3oz) raisins
2 × 400g cans chickpeas, drained and rinsed
ground black pepper
plain naan or pitta bread to serve

1. Heat a large wide non-stick pan. Add the chicken pieces and fry until well browned all over. Add the butter and, when melted, add the onion and garlic. Cook, stirring, for 5 minutes.

2. Add the harissa, saffron, salt and cinnamon stick, then season well with pepper. Pour in the stock and bring to the boil. Reduce the heat, cover the pan and simmer gently for 25–30 minutes.

3. Add the raisins and chickpeas and bring to the boil, then reduce the heat and simmer uncovered for 5–10 minutes.

4. Serve with warm flatbread such as plain naan or pitta.

FREEZING TIP

To freeze Freeze leftover portions separately. Complete the recipe, then cool quickly. Put into a sealable container and freeze for up to three months.
To use Thaw overnight in the fridge. Put into a pan, cover and bring to the boil. Reduce the heat to low, then reheat for 40 minutes or until the chicken is hot right through.

Spiced One-pot Chicken

Preparation Time 10 minutes, plus marinating • Cooking Time 1 hour 10 minutes • Serves 6 • Per Serving 604 calories, 36g fat (of which 10g saturates), 20g carbohydrate, 0.5g salt • Gluten Free • Dairy Free • Easy

3 tbsp Thai red curry paste
150ml (¼ pint) orange juice
2 garlic cloves, crushed
6 chicken pieces, 2.3kg (5lb) total weight, with bone in
700g (1½lb) squash or pumpkin, peeled and cut into 5cm (2in) cubes
5 red onions, quartered
2 tbsp capers, drained and chopped
salt and ground black pepper

1. Combine the curry paste, orange juice and garlic in a bowl. Put the chicken pieces in the marinade and leave to marinate for 15 minutes.

2. Preheat the oven to 220°C (200°C fan oven) mark 7. Put the vegetables into a large roasting tin, then remove the chicken from the marinade and arrange on top of the vegetables. Pour the marinade over and season with salt and pepper. Mix everything together to cover with the marinade, then scatter with the capers.

3. Cook for 1 hour 10 minutes, turning from time to time, or until the chicken is cooked through and the skin is golden.

GET AHEAD

To prepare ahead Complete the recipe to the end of step 2. Cover and chill for up to one day.
To use Complete the recipe, but cook for a further 5–10 minutes.

Caribbean Chicken

Preparation Time 40 minutes, plus marinating • Cooking Time 45–50 minutes • Serves 5 •
Per Serving 617 calories, 39g fat (of which 12g saturates), 25g carbohydrate, 2.1g salt • Easy

10 chicken pieces, such as thighs, drumsticks, wings or breasts, skinned
1 tsp salt
1 tbsp ground coriander
2 tsp ground cumin
1 tbsp paprika
a pinch of ground nutmeg
1 fresh Scotch bonnet or other hot red chilli, seeded and chopped (see page 30)
1 onion, chopped
5 fresh thyme sprigs
4 garlic cloves, crushed
2 tbsp dark soy sauce
juice of 1 lemon
2 tbsp vegetable oil
2 tbsp light muscovado sugar

350g (12oz) American easy-cook rice
3 tbsp dark rum (optional)
25g (1oz) butter
2 × 300g cans black-eye beans, drained
ground black pepper
a few fresh thyme sprigs to garnish

1. Pierce the chicken pieces with a knife, put into a container and sprinkle with ½ tsp salt, some pepper, the coriander, cumin, paprika and nutmeg. Add the chilli, onion, thyme leaves and garlic. Pour the soy sauce and lemon juice over and stir to combine. Cover and chill for at least 4 hours.

2. Heat a 3.4 litre (6 pint) heavy-based pan over a medium heat for 2 minutes. Add the oil and sugar and cook for 3 minutes or until it turns a golden caramel colour. (Don't overcook it as the mixture will blacken and taste burnt – watch it closely.) Remove the chicken from the marinade. Add to the caramel mixture. Cover and cook over a medium heat for 5 minutes. Turn the chicken and cook, covered, for another 5 minutes or until evenly browned. Add the onion mixture and any marinade juices. Turn again, then re-cover and cook for 10 minutes.

3. Add the rice and stir to combine with the chicken, then pour in 900ml (1½ pints) cold water. Add the rum, if using, the butter and the remaining ½ tsp salt. Cover and simmer over a gentle heat, without lifting the lid, for 20 minutes or until the rice is tender and most of the liquid has been absorbed.

4. Add the black-eye beans to the pan and mix well. Cover the pan and cook for 3–5 minutes until the beans are warmed through and all the liquid has been absorbed, taking care that the rice doesn't stick to the bottom of the pan. Garnish with the thyme sprigs and serve hot.

Chicken Curry

Preparation Time 20–25 minutes • Cooking Time about 50 minutes • Serves 4 • Per Serving 342 calories,
10g fat (of which 2g saturates), 25g carbohydrate, 0.5g salt • Gluten Free • Dairy Free • Easy

1 tbsp oil

4 chicken legs, skinned

1 onion, finely chopped

2 tbsp mild or medium curry paste

2 leeks, trimmed and sliced

200g can chopped tomatoes

1 small cauliflower, broken into
**   florets**

250g (9oz) small new potatoes

600ml (1 pint) hot chicken stock

150g (5oz) each spinach and
**   frozen peas**

naan bread or rice (optional)
**   to serve**

1. Heat the oil in a large non-stick casserole dish and brown the chicken all over. After 5 minutes, add the onion to the pan and cook for 5–10 minutes until golden.

2. Add the curry paste and cook for 1 minute, then add the leeks, tomatoes, cauliflower, potatoes and hot stock. Bring to the boil, then reduce the heat, cover the pan and simmer for 20–30 minutes until the chicken is cooked and the potatoes are tender.

3. Add the spinach and peas and cook for 5 minutes or until heated through. Serve with naan bread, or rice, if you like.

Chicken & Pork Terrine

Preparation Time 30 minutes, plus overnight chilling • Cooking Time about 2 hours 10 minutes, plus cooling •
Serves 8 • Per Serving 332 calories, 21g fat (of which 6g saturates), 6g carbohydrate, 1.3g salt • A Little Effort

1 tbsp olive oil, plus extra to brush

1 onion, finely chopped

2 tbsp brandy (optional)

12 smoked streaky bacon rashers

2 skinless chicken breasts, cut into 1cm (½in) pieces (or use turkey breast or mince)

500g pack of pork mince

50g (2oz) pistachios, roughly chopped

50g (2oz) dried cranberries

¾ tsp freshly grated nutmeg

2 fresh thyme sprigs, leaves picked off

salt and freshly ground black pepper

fruit chutney and toast to serve

1. Heat the oil in a medium pan and cook the onion gently for 10 minutes or until softened. Carefully add the brandy, if you like, and bubble for 30 seconds, then tip the mixture into a large bowl and leave to cool.

2. Preheat the oven to 180°C (160°C fan oven) mark 4. Use about 10 of the bacon rashers to line the inside of a 900g (2lb) loaf tin, leaving the excess hanging over the sides. Add the chopped chicken, pork, pistachios, cranberries, nutmeg, thyme leaves and plenty of seasoning (it needs a fair amount of salt) to the cooled onion mixture and mix well.

3. Press the mixture into the prepared loaf tin and level the surface. Fold any overhanging bacon over the filling and cover with the remaining rashers. Press down again to make sure the surface is smooth. Lightly oil a small sheet of foil and press on top of the loaf tin. Wrap the tin well in a further double layer of foil, then put into a roasting tin. Half-fill the roasting tin with boiling water from the kettle and carefully transfer to the oven.

4. Cook for 1½ hours or until the terrine feels solid when pressed. Lift the tin out of the water. Unwrap the outer layers of foil (leaving the greased foil layer in place). Carefully pour out any liquid from the terrine (this will set into a jelly if not done). Leave to cool.

5. Sit the loaf tin on a baking tray and place three cans of tomatoes (or similar) on top of the terrine (resting on the foil layer). Chill overnight.

6. When ready to serve, preheat the oven to 200°C (180°C fan oven) mark 6. Unmould the terrine on to a baking tray and lightly brush with oil. Brown in the oven for 20–25 minutes (if you don't want the terrine browned, leave this step out). Serve the terrine warm or at room temperature in slices, with fruit chutney and toast.

GET AHEAD

Prepare the terrine to the end of step 5 up to two days ahead. Remove the weights and chill again. Complete the recipe to serve.

Clementine & Sage Turkey with Madeira Gravy

Preparation Time 30 minutes • Cooking Time about 3 hours 40 minutes, plus resting • Serves 8, with leftovers •
Per Serving (with stuffing) 301 calories, 19g fat (of which 9g saturates), 12g carbohydrate, 0.9g salt • A Little Effort

5.4kg (12lb) free-range turkey
  (keep the giblets for stock, if you
  like to one side). Spend as much
  as you can on your turkey – you'll
  notice the difference in the
  texture and taste)
3 firm clementines
20g pack of fresh sage
100g (3½oz) butter, softened
500g (1lb 2oz) stuffing (see
  pages 222–3)
3 celery sticks
3 carrots, halved lengthways
salt and freshly ground black
  pepper
fried clementine halves and
  stuffing balls to garnish
  (optional)

FOR THE MADEIRA GRAVY
25g (1oz) plain flour
125ml (4fl oz) Madeira wine
300ml (½ pint) chicken stock
1 tbsp runny honey or redcurrant
  jelly, if needed

1. Remove the turkey from the fridge 1 hour before you stuff it to let it come up to room temperature.

2. Preheat the oven to 190°C (170°C fan oven) mark 5. Finely grate the zest from the clementines into a medium bowl. Halve the zest-free clementines and put to one side. Next, add 2 tbsp thinly sliced sage leaves (keep the rest of the bunch to one side) to the bowl with the butter and plenty of seasoning and mix well.

3. Put the turkey, breast side up, on a board. Use tweezers to pluck any feathers from the skin. Loosen the skin at the neck end and use your fingers to ease the skin away from the breast meat, until 9cm (3½in) is free. Spread most of the butter between the skin and meat. Put the remaining flavoured butter to one side.

4. Spoon the cold stuffing into the neck cavity, pushing it down between the skin and breast meat and taking care not to overfill. Neaten the shape. Turn the turkey over on to its breast, pull the neck flap down and over the stuffing and secure the neck skin with a skewer or cocktail sticks. Weigh the turkey and calculate the cooking time, allowing 30–35 minutes per 1kg (2¼lb).

5. Make a platform in a large roasting tin with celery sticks and carrot halves and sit the turkey on top. Put the clementine halves and the remaining sage (sticks and all) into the turkey cavity, then rub the remaining flavoured butter over the breast of the bird. Tie the legs together with string, season the bird all over and cover loosely with foil.

6. Roast for the calculated time, removing the foil for the last 45 minutes of cooking, and basting at least three times during cooking. If the skin is browning too quickly, cover with foil again.

7. To check if the turkey is cooked, pierce the thickest part of the thigh with a skewer – the juices should run clear. If there are any traces of pink in the juice, put the bird back into the oven and cook for 10 minutes, then check again in the same way. Alternatively, use a meat thermometer – the temperature needs to read 78°C when inserted into the thickest part of the breast.

8. When the turkey is cooked, tip the bird so that the juices run into the tin, then transfer the turkey to a board (put the tin for the Madeira Gravy to one side). Cover loosely with foil and clean teatowels to help keep the heat in. Leave to rest in a warm place for 30 minutes–1¼ hours.

9. To make the gravy, spoon off most of the fat from the roasting tin (leaving the vegetables in the tin). Put the tin over a medium heat and add the flour. Cook, stirring well with a wooden spoon, for 1 minute. Gradually add the Madeira, scraping up all the sticky bits from the bottom of the tin, then leave to bubble for a few minutes. Next, stir in the stock and leave to simmer, stirring occasionally, for 5 minutes. Check the seasoning and add the honey or redcurrant jelly if needed. Strain into a warmed gravy jug.

10. To serve, unwrap the turkey and transfer to a warmed plate. Remove the skewer or cocktail sticks. Garnish with the clementine halves and stuffing balls. Serve with the gravy.

Lemon & Parsley Butter Roast Turkey

Preparation Time 25 minutes • Cooking Time about 3½ hours, plus resting • Serves 8, with leftovers •
Per Serving 286 calories, 11g fat (of which 5g saturates), 28g carbohydrate, 0.6g salt • A Little Effort

5.4kg (12lb) free-range turkey

1 lemon, zested (put the lemon to one side)

100g (3½oz) unsalted butter, softened

20g pack of fresh flat-leafed parsley, finely chopped

500g (1lb 2oz) uncooked Herbed Bread Stuffing (see page 223)

1 red onion, halved

5 fresh bay leaves (optional)

salt and freshly ground black pepper

fresh bay leaves and extra lemon halves browned (cut side down) in oil to garnish (optional)

1. Remove the turkey from the fridge 1 hour before you stuff it to let it come up to room temperature.

2. Preheat the oven to 190°C (170°C fan oven) mark 5. Put the lemon zest, butter, parsley and plenty of seasoning into a small bowl and mix well.

3. Put the turkey, breast side up, on a board. Use tweezers to pluck any feathers from the skin. Loosen the skin at the neck end and use your fingers to ease the skin gently away from breast meat, until about 9cm (3½in) is free. Spread the butter mixture between the skin and meat.

4. Spoon the cold stuffing into the neck cavity, pushing it down between the skin and breast meat and taking care not to overfill. Neaten the shape. Turn the turkey over on to its breast, pull the neck flap down and over the stuffing and secure the neck skin with a skewer or cocktail sticks. Weigh the turkey and calculate the cooking time, allowing 30–35 minutes per 1kg (2¼lb).

5. Transfer the turkey to a large roasting tin. Cut the zested lemon in half and squeeze the juice over the bird. Put the juiced halves into the bird's cavity, together with the red onion halves and the bay leaves, if you like. Tie the legs together with string, season the bird all over and cover loosely with foil.

6. Roast for the calculated time, removing the foil for the last 30 minutes of cooking, and basting at least four times during cooking. If the skin is browning too quickly, cover with foil again.

7. To check if the turkey is cooked, pierce the thickest part of the thigh with a skewer – the juices should run clear. If there are any traces of pink in the juice, put the bird back into the oven and cook for 10 minutes, then check again in the same way. Alternatively, use a meat thermometer – the temperature needs to read 78°C when inserted into thickest part of the breast.

8. When the turkey is cooked, tip the bird so that the juices run into the tin, then transfer the turkey to a board (put the roasting tin for the gravy to one side). Cover well with foil and clean teatowels to help keep the heat in, then leave to rest in a warm place for 30 minutes–1¼ hours.

9. When ready to serve, put on a warmed plate or board, remove the string, skewer or cocktail sticks and garnish with bay leaves and lemon, if you like.

Goose with Roasted Apples

Preparation Time 30 minutes • Cooking Time 3 hours, plus resting • Serves 6–8 •
Per Serving 646 calories, 41g fat (of which 12g saturates), 11g carbohydrate, 1g salt • Easy

6 small red onions, halved

**7 small red eating apples,
    unpeeled, halved**

**5kg (11lb) oven-ready goose, dried
    and seasoned inside and out**

1 small bunch of fresh sage

1 small bunch of fresh rosemary

1 bay leaf

**salt and freshly ground black
    pepper**

FOR THE GRAVY
1 tbsp plain flour
300ml (½ pint) red wine
200ml (7fl oz) giblet stock

1. Preheat the oven to 230°C (210°C fan oven) mark 8. Put half an onion and half an apple inside the goose with half the sage and rosemary and the bay leaf. Tie the legs together with string. Push a long skewer through the wings to tuck them in. Put the goose, breast side up, on a rack in a roasting tin. Prick the breast all over and season with salt and ground black pepper. Put the remaining onions around the bird, then cover loosely with foil.

2. Roast in the oven for 30 minutes, then take the tin out of the oven and baste the goose with the fat that has run off. Remove and put any excess fat to one side. Reduce the oven temperature to 190°C (170°C fan oven) mark 5 and roast for a further 1½ hours, removing any excess fat every 20–30 minutes.

3. Remove the foil from the goose. Remove excess fat from the tin, then add the remaining apples. Sprinkle the goose with the remaining herbs and roast for a further 1 hour or until cooked. To test if the bird is cooked, pierce the thickest part of the thigh with a skewer – the juices should run clear. If there are any traces of pink in the juice, put the bird back into the oven and cook for 10 minutes, then check again in the same way. Alternatively, use a meat thermometer – the temperature needs to read 78°C when inserted into the thickest part of the breast.

4. Take the goose out of the oven and put it on a warmed serving plate. Cover with foil and leave to rest for 30 minutes. Remove the apples and onions and keep warm.

5. To make the gravy, pour out all but 1 tbsp of the fat from the tin, stir in the flour, then add the wine and stock. Bring to the boil and cook, stirring, for 5 minutes.

6. Carve the goose, cut the roast apples into wedges and serve with the goose, onions and gravy.

Pot-roasted Pheasant with Red Cabbage

Preparation Time 15 minutes • Cooking Time about 1 hour • Serves 4 • Per Serving 659 calories, 21g fat (of which 12g saturates), 11g carbohydrate, 1.4g salt • Gluten Free • Easy

25g (1oz) butter
1 tbsp oil
2 oven-ready young pheasants, halved
2 onions, sliced
450g (1lb) red cabbage, cored and finely shredded

1 tsp cornflour
250ml (9fl oz) red wine
2 tbsp redcurrant jelly
1 tbsp balsamic vinegar
4 rindless smoked streaky bacon rashers, halved
salt and ground black pepper

1. Preheat the oven to 200°C (180°C fan oven) mark 6. Melt the butter with the oil in a large flameproof casserole over a medium to high heat. Add the pheasant and brown on all sides, then remove and put to one side. Add the onions and cabbage to the casserole and fry for 5 minutes, stirring frequently, or until softened.

2. Blend the cornflour with a little water to make a paste. Add to the casserole with the wine, redcurrant jelly and vinegar. Season with salt and pepper. Bring to the boil, stirring.

3. Arrange the pheasant halves, skin side up, on the cabbage. Put the halved bacon rashers on top. Cover the casserole and cook in the oven for 30 minutes or until the birds are tender (older pheasants would take an extra 10–20 minutes).

4. Serve the pot-roasted pheasant and red cabbage with the cooking juices spooned over.

TRY SOMETHING DIFFERENT
Pot-roasted Pigeon with Red Cabbage
Instead of the pheasant, use oven-ready pigeons; put an onion wedge inside each bird before browning to impart extra flavour.

Rabbit Casserole with Prunes

Preparation Time 20 minutes, plus soaking • Cooking Time 1¼ hours • Serves 6 • Per Serving 538 calories, 26g fat (of which 13g saturates), 11g carbohydrate, 0.5g salt • Gluten Free • Easy

- 175g (6oz) ready-to-eat pitted prunes
- 300ml (½ pint) red wine
- 3–4 tbsp olive oil
- about 2.3kg (5lb) rabbit joints
- 1 large onion, chopped
- 2 large garlic cloves, crushed
- 5 tbsp Armagnac
- 450ml (¾ pint) light stock
- a few fresh thyme sprigs, tied together, or 1 tsp dried thyme, plus extra sprigs to garnish
- 2 bay leaves
- 150ml (½ pint) double cream
- 125g (4oz) brown-cap mushrooms, sliced
- salt and ground black pepper

1. Put the prunes and wine into a bowl. Cover and leave for about 4 hours, then strain, keeping the wine and prunes to one side.

2. Preheat the oven to 170°C (150°C fan oven) mark 3. Heat 3 tbsp oil in a flameproof casserole. Brown the rabbit joints a few at a time, then remove from the casserole. Add the onion and garlic with a little more oil, if needed, and brown lightly. Put the rabbit back into the casserole, add the Armagnac and warm through. Carefully light the Armagnac with a taper or long match, then shake the pan gently until the flames subside.

3. Pour in the stock and the wine from the prunes and bring to the boil. Add the thyme sprigs or dried thyme to the casserole with the bay leaves and plenty of salt and pepper. Cover tightly and cook in the oven for about 1 hour or until tender.

4. Lift the rabbit out of the juices and keep warm. Boil the cooking juices until reduced by half. Add the cream and mushrooms and continue boiling for 2–3 minutes. Stir in the prunes and warm through. Adjust the seasoning, then spoon the sauce over the rabbit to serve. Garnish with sprigs of fresh thyme.

TRY SOMETHING DIFFERENT
Use chicken joints instead of rabbit.

Braised Guinea Fowl & Red Cabbage

Preparation Time 30 minutes • Cooking Time 2 hours 20 minutes • Serves 8 • Per Serving 373 calories, 17g fat (of which 6g saturates), 12g carbohydrate, 0.9g salt • Dairy Free • Easy

2 tbsp rapeseed oil
2 oven-ready guinea fowl
150g (5oz) smoked lardons
400g (14oz) whole shallots, peeled
1 small red cabbage, cored and
    finely sliced
12 juniper berries, crushed
2 tsp dark brown sugar
1 tbsp red wine vinegar
2 fresh thyme sprigs
150ml (¼ pint) hot chicken stock
salt and ground black pepper

1. Preheat the oven to 180°C (160°C fan oven) mark 4. Heat 1 tbsp oil in a flameproof casserole large enough for both birds and brown the guinea fowl over a medium to high heat. Remove from the casserole and set aside.

2. Add the remaining oil to the casserole with the lardons. Fry gently to release the fat, then add the shallots and cook over a medium heat until lightly browned.

3. Stir in the red cabbage and cook for 5 minutes, stirring, or until the cabbage has softened slightly. Add the juniper berries, sugar, vinegar, thyme and hot stock. Season with salt and pepper.

4. Put the guinea fowl on top of the cabbage mixture, then cover the casserole tightly with a lid or double thickness of foil and braise in the oven for 1½ hours. Remove the lid and continue cooking for 30 minutes or until the birds are cooked through – the juices should run clear when you pierce the thighs with a skewer.

5. Transfer the guinea fowl to a board and spoon the cabbage and juices on to a serving platter. Keep warm. Joint the birds into eight, as you would a chicken, then arrange the guinea fowl on the platter on top of the cabbage. Serve at once.

Peppered Winter Stew

Preparation Time 20 minutes • Cooking Time 2¾ hours • Serves 6 • Per Serving 540 calories, 24g fat
(of which 7g saturates), 24g carbohydrate, 1.5g salt • Dairy Free • Easy

25g (1oz) plain flour
900g (2lb) stewing venison, beef or
    lamb, cut into 4cm (1½in) cubes
5 tbsp oil
225g (8oz) button onions or shallots,
    peeled with root end intact
225g (8oz) onion, finely chopped
4 garlic cloves, crushed
2 tbsp tomato purée
125ml (4fl oz) red wine vinegar
750ml bottle red wine
2 tbsp redcurrant jelly
1 small bunch of fresh thyme, plus
    extra sprigs to garnish (optional)
4 bay leaves
6 cloves
900g (2lb) mixed root vegetables,
    such as carrots, parsnips,
    turnips and celeriac, cut into
    4cm (1½in) chunks; carrots cut
    a little smaller
600–900ml (1–1½ pints) beef stock
salt and ground black pepper

1. Preheat the oven to 180°C (160°C fan oven) mark 4. Put the flour into a plastic bag, season with salt and pepper, then toss the meat in it.

2. Heat 3 tbsp oil in a large flameproof casserole over a medium heat and brown the meat well in small batches. Remove and put to one side.

3. Heat the remaining oil and fry the button onions or shallots for 5 minutes or until golden. Add the chopped onion and the garlic and cook, stirring, until soft and golden. Add the tomato purée and cook for a further 2 minutes, then add the vinegar and wine and bring to the boil. Bubble for 10 minutes.

4. Add the redcurrant jelly, thyme, bay leaves, 1 tbsp coarsely ground black pepper, the cloves and meat to the pan, with the vegetables and enough stock to barely cover the meat and vegetables. Bring to the boil, then reduce the heat, cover the pan and cook in the oven for 1¾–2¼ hours until the meat is very tender. Serve hot, garnished with thyme sprigs, if you like.

FREEZING TIP

To freeze Complete the recipe to the end of step 4, without the garnish. Cool quickly and put in a freezerproof container. Seal and freeze for up to one month.
To use Thaw overnight at cool room temperature. Preheat the oven to 180°C (160°C fan oven) mark 4. Put into a flameproof casserole and add an extra 150ml (¼ pint) beef stock. Bring to the boil. Cover and reheat for 30 minutes.

Poacher's Pie

Preparation Time 20 minutes, plus chilling • Cooking Time 1½ hours • Serves 4 •
Per Serving 692 calories, 37g fat (of which 16g saturates), 57g carbohydrate, 1.8g salt • A Little Effort

**225g (8oz) plain flour, plus extra to
dust**
50g (2oz) butter
50g (2oz) lard
**450g (1lb) boneless rabbit, skinned
and cubed**
**125g (4oz) streaky bacon rashers,
rind removed and chopped**
**2 medium potatoes, peeled and
sliced**
**1 medium leek, trimmed and
sliced**
**1 tbsp freshly chopped flat-leafed
parsley**
¼ tsp mixed dried herbs
chicken stock
1 medium egg, beaten, to glaze
salt and ground black pepper

1. Preheat the oven to 190°C (170°C fan oven) mark 5. Put the flour and a pinch of salt into a bowl and rub in the butter and lard until the mixture resembles fine breadcrumbs. Add 3–4 tbsp cold water and mix to form a firm dough. Chill for 30 minutes.

2. Fill a 1.7 litre (3 pint) pie dish with alternate layers of rabbit, bacon and vegetables, sprinkling with seasoning and herbs. Half-fill the dish with stock.

3. Roll out the pastry on a lightly floured surface to 5cm (2in) wider than the top of the dish. Cut a 2.5cm (1in) strip from the outer edge and line the dampened rim of the dish.

Dampen the pastry rim and cover with the pastry lid. Trim and seal the edges. Make a hole in the centre to let the steam escape. Decorate with pastry leaves made from the trimmings and brush with beaten egg.

4. Cook in the oven for 30 minutes. Cover loosely with foil, then reduce the oven temperature to 180°C (160°C fan oven) mark 4 and cook for a further 1 hour. Serve hot.

MEAT

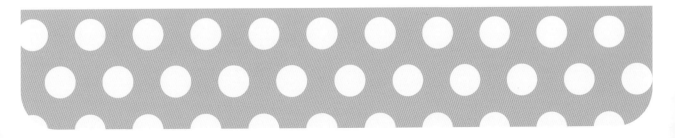

Beef Casserole with Black Olives

Preparation Time 20 minutes • Cooking Time 2 hours 10 minutes • Serves 6 • Per Serving 704 calories, 45g fat (of which 13g saturates), 9g carbohydrate, 3.3g salt • Dairy Free • Easy

6 tbsp oil

1.1kg (2½lb) stewing steak, cut into 4cm (1½in) cubes

350g (12oz) unsmoked streaky bacon rashers, rind removed and sliced into thin strips

450g (1lb) onions, roughly chopped

3 large garlic cloves

2 tbsp tomato purée

125ml (4fl oz) brandy

1 tbsp plain flour

150ml (¼ pint) red wine

300ml (½ pint) beef stock

1 bouquet garni

225g (8oz) flat mushrooms, quartered if large

125g (4oz) black olives

fresh flat-leafed parsley sprigs to garnish (optional)

1. Heat 3 tbsp oil in a large flameproof casserole over a high heat. Brown the steak in batches until dark chestnut brown; remove and keep warm. Add the bacon and fry until golden brown, then put to one side with the beef.

2. Add the remaining oil and cook the onions over a medium heat for 10–15 minutes until golden. Add the garlic, fry for 30 seconds, then add the tomato purée and cook, stirring, for 1–2 minutes. Add the brandy.

3. Preheat the oven to 170°C (150°C fan oven) mark 3. Bring the casserole to the boil and bubble to reduce by half, then add the flour and mix until smooth. Pour in the wine, bring back to the boil and bubble for 1 minute. Put the steak and bacon back into the casserole, then add enough stock to barely cover the meat. Add the bouquet garni. Bring to the boil, then cover, put into the oven and cook for 1¼–1½ hours until the steak is tender. Add the mushrooms and cook for a further 4–5 minutes.

4. Just before serving, remove the bouquet garni and stir in the black olives. Serve hot, garnished with parsley, if you like.

FREEZING TIP

To freeze Complete the recipe to the end of step 3. Cool quickly and put into a freezerproof container. Seal and freeze for up to one month. *To use* Thaw overnight at cool room temperature. Preheat the oven to 180°C (160°C fan oven) mark 4. Bring slowly to the boil on the hob, then cover and reheat in the oven for 20–25 minutes. Complete the recipe.

Beef Jambalaya

Preparation Time 10 minutes • Cooking Time 40 minutes • Serves 4 • Per Serving 554 calories,
30g fat (of which 9g saturates), 40g carbohydrate, 1.8g salt • Gluten Free • Dairy Free • Easy

**275g (10oz) fillet steak, cut into
   thin strips**
4 tsp mild chilli powder
1 tsp ground black pepper
about 5 tbsp oil
**150g (5oz) chorizo sausage,
   sliced and cut into strips, or
   125g (4oz) cubed**
**2 celery sticks, cut into 5cm
   (2in) strips**
**2 red peppers, seeded and cut into
   5cm (2in) strips**
150g (5oz) onions, roughly chopped
2 garlic cloves, crushed
275g (10oz) long-grain white rice

1 tbsp tomato purée
1 tbsp ground ginger
2 tsp Cajun spice mix
900ml (1½ pints) beef stock
**8 large cooked prawns,
   peeled and deveined
   (see page 57)**
salt
mixed salad to serve

1. Put the steak into a plastic
bag with 1 tsp chilli powder and
the black pepper, seal and shake
to mix.

2. Heat 1 tbsp oil in a large
heavy-based frying pan and
cook the chorizo until golden. Add
the celery and red peppers to the
pan and cook for 3–4 minutes until
just beginning to soften and brown.
Remove from the pan and put to
one side. Add 2 tbsp oil to the pan
and fry the steak in batches; put
to one side and keep warm.

3. Add a little more oil to the pan,
if needed, and cook the onion until
transparent. Add the garlic, rice,
tomato purée, remaining chilli
powder, ground ginger and Cajun
spice mix, then cook for 2 minutes
or until the rice turns translucent.
Stir in the stock, season with salt
and bring to the boil. Reduce the
heat, cover the pan and simmer
for about 20 minutes, stirring
occasionally, or until the rice is
tender and most of the liquid has
been absorbed (add a little more
water during cooking if needed).

4. Add the reserved steak, chorizo,
red peppers and celery and the
prawns. Heat gently, stirring, until
piping hot. Adjust the seasoning
and serve with a mixed salad.

COOK'S TIP
*Jambalaya is a rice-based dish from
Louisiana that traditionally contains
spicy sausage, chicken, ham or
prawns and lots of chilli pepper.*

Chunky One-pot Bolognese

Preparation Time 15 minutes • Cooking Time about 1 hour • Serves 6 • Per Serving 506 calories, 31g fat (of which 11g saturates), 40g carbohydrate, 1.5g salt • Dairy Free • Easy

3 tbsp olive oil
2 large red onions, finely diced
a few fresh rosemary sprigs
1 large aubergine, finely diced
8 plump coarse sausages
350ml (12fl oz) full-bodied red wine
700g (1½lb) passata
4 tbsp sun-dried tomato paste
300ml (½ pint) hot vegetable stock
175g (6oz) small dried pasta, such as orecchiette
salt and ground black pepper

1. Heat 2 tbsp oil in a large shallow non-stick pan. Add the onions and rosemary and cook over a gentle heat for 10 minutes or until soft and golden.

2. Add the aubergine and remaining oil and cook over a medium heat for 8–10 minutes until soft and golden.

3. Meanwhile, pull the skin off the sausages and divide each into four rough chunks. Tip the aubergine mixture on to a plate and add the sausage chunks to the hot pan. You won't need any extra oil.

4. Stir the sausage pieces over a high heat for 6–8 minutes until golden and beginning to turn crisp at the edges. Pour in the wine and allow to bubble for 6–8 minutes until only a little liquid remains. Put the aubergine mixture back into the pan, along with the passata, tomato paste and hot stock.

5. Stir the pasta into the liquid, cover, then simmer for 20 minutes or until the pasta is cooked. Taste and season with salt and pepper if necessary.

FREEZING TIP

To freeze *Freeze leftover portions separately. Complete the recipe to the end of step 4. Add the pasta and cook for 10 minutes – it will continue to cook right through when you reheat the Bolognese. Cool, put into a freezerproof container and freeze for up to three months.*
To use *Thaw overnight at cool room temperature, put into a pan and add 150ml (¼ pint) water. Bring to the boil, then simmer gently for 10 minutes or until the sauce is hot and the pasta is cooked.*

Braised Beef with Pancetta & Mushrooms

Preparation Time 20 minutes • Cooking Time about 3½ hours • Serves 4 • Per Serving 541 calories, 25g fat (of which 9g saturates), 30g carbohydrate, 1.6g salt • Dairy Free • Easy

175g (6oz) smoked pancetta or smoked streaky bacon, cubed
2 leeks, trimmed and thickly sliced
1 tbsp olive oil
450g (1lb) braising steak, cut into 5cm (2in) pieces
1 large onion, finely chopped
2 carrots, thickly sliced
2 parsnips, thickly sliced
1 tbsp plain flour
300ml (½ pint) red wine
1–2 tbsp redcurrant jelly
125g (4oz) chestnut mushrooms, halved
ground black pepper
freshly chopped flat-leafed parsley to garnish

1. Preheat the oven to 170°C (150°C fan oven) mark 3. Fry the pancetta or bacon in a flameproof casserole for 2–3 minutes until golden. Add the leeks and cook for a further 2 minutes or until they are just beginning to colour. Remove with a slotted spoon and set aside.

2. Heat the oil in the casserole. Fry the beef in batches for 2–3 minutes until golden brown on all sides. Remove and set aside. Add the onion and fry over a gentle heat for 5 minutes or until golden. Stir in the carrots and parsnips and fry for 1–2 minutes.

3. Put the beef back into the casserole and stir in the flour to soak up the juices. Gradually add the wine and 300ml (½ pint) water, then stir in the redcurrant jelly. Season with pepper and bring to the boil. Cover with a tight-fitting lid and cook in the oven for 2 hours.

4. Stir in the leeks, pancetta and mushrooms, cover and cook for a further 1 hour or until everything is tender. Serve hot, sprinkled with chopped parsley.

FREEZING TIP

To freeze Complete the recipe to the end of step 4, without the garnish. Put into a freezerproof container, cool and freeze for up to three months.
To use Thaw overnight at cool room temperature. Preheat the oven to 180°C (160°C fan oven) mark 4. Bring to the boil on the hob, cover tightly and reheat in the oven for about 30 minutes or until piping hot.

One-pot Spicy Beef

Preparation Time 10 minutes • Cooking Time about 40 minutes • Serves 4 • Per Serving 380 calories, 13g fat (of which 8g saturates), 36g carbohydrate, 1.8g salt • Gluten Free • Dairy Free • Easy

2 tsp sunflower oil

1 large onion, roughly chopped

1 garlic clove, finely chopped

1 small red chilli, finely chopped (see page 30)

2 red peppers, seeded and roughly chopped

2 celery sticks, diced

400g (14oz) lean beef mince

400g can chopped tomatoes

2 × 400g cans mixed beans, drained and rinsed

1–2 tsp Tabasco sauce

salsa to serve (see Cook's Tip)

1. Heat the oil in a large frying pan. Add the onion to the pan with 2 tbsp water and cook for 10 minutes or until softened. Add the garlic and chilli and cook for 1–2 minutes until golden, then add the red peppers and celery and cook for 5 minutes.

2. Add the beef to the pan and brown all over. Add the tomatoes, beans and Tabasco, then simmer for 20 minutes. Serve with the salsa.

COOK'S TIP

Salsa

Put ½ ripe avocado, peeled and roughly chopped, 4 roughly chopped tomatoes, 1 tsp olive oil and the juice of ½ lime into a bowl and stir well. Serve at once.

Braised Beef with Mustard & Capers

Preparation Time 15 minutes • Cooking Time 2 hours 20 minutes, plus cooling • Serves 4 • Per Serving 391 calories, 19g fat (of which 7g saturates), 10g carbohydrate, 1.5g salt • Gluten Free • Dairy Free • Easy

50g (2oz) can anchovy fillets in oil, drained, chopped and oil put to one side
olive oil
700g (1½lb) braising steak, cut into small strips
2 large Spanish onions, peeled and thinly sliced
2 tbsp capers
1 tsp English mustard
6 fresh thyme sprigs
20g pack fresh flat-leafed parsley, roughly chopped
salt and ground black pepper
green salad and crusty bread or mashed potato to serve

1. Preheat the oven to 170°C (150°C fan oven) mark 3. Measure the anchovy oil into a deep flameproof casserole, then make up to 3 tbsp with the olive oil. Heat the oil and fry the meat, a few pieces at a time, until well browned. Remove with a slotted spoon and set aside. When all the meat has been browned, pour 4 tbsp cold water into the empty casserole and stir to loosen any bits on the bottom.

2. Put the meat back into the pan and add the onions, anchovies, capers, mustard, half the thyme and all but 1 tbsp of the parsley. Stir until thoroughly mixed.

3. Tear off a sheet of greaseproof paper big enough to cover the pan. Crumple it up and wet it under the cold tap. Squeeze out most of the water, open it out and press down over the surface of the meat.

4. Cover with a tight-fitting lid and cook in the oven for 2 hours or until the beef is meltingly tender. Check the casserole after 1 hour to make sure it's still moist. If it looks dry, add a little water.

5. Adjust for seasoning, then stir in the remaining parsley and thyme. Serve with a green salad and crusty bread or mashed potato.

COOK'S TIP
To make a deliciously easy mash, put four baking potatoes into the oven when you put in the casserole. Leave to bake for 2 hours. Cut each potato in half and use a fork to scrape out the flesh into a bowl. Add 50g (2oz) butter and season well with salt and pepper – the potato will be soft enough to mash with the fork.

Braised Beef with Chestnuts & Celery

Preparation Time 25 minutes • Cooking Time 2¼ hours • Serves 6 • Per Serving 336 calories, 16g fat (of which 6g saturates), 12g carbohydrate, 1.3g salt • Easy

18 fresh chestnuts, skins split

15g (½oz) butter

1 tbsp vegetable oil

2 bacon rashers, rind removed, chopped

900g (2lb) stewing steak, cubed

1 medium onion, chopped

1 tbsp plain flour

300ml (½ pint) brown ale

300ml (½ pint) beef stock

a pinch of freshly grated nutmeg

finely grated zest and juice of 1 orange

3 celery sticks, chopped

salt and freshly ground black pepper

freshly chopped flat-leafed parsley to garnish

1. Preheat the oven to 170°C (150°C fan oven) mark 3. Cook the chestnuts in simmering water for about 7 minutes. Remove from the water one at a time and peel off the thick outer skin and thin inner skin while still warm.

2. Heat the butter and oil in a flameproof casserole. Add the bacon and beef in batches and cook, stirring occasionally, until browned. Remove the meat with a slotted spoon.

3. Add the onion to the casserole and fry, stirring, until softened. Drain off most of the fat. Put the meat back into the casserole, sprinkle in the flour and cook, stirring, for 1–2 minutes.

4. Stir in the brown ale, stock, nutmeg, orange juice and half the zest and season to taste. Bring to the boil, then stir well to loosen the sediment and add the chestnuts. Cover tightly with foil and a lid and cook in the oven for about 45 minutes.

5. After 45 minutes, add the celery to the casserole and cook for a further 1 hour or until the meat is tender. Serve with the remaining orange zest and the parsley sprinkled over the top.

Smoky Pimento Goulash

Preparation Time 20 minutes • Cooking Time about 3 hours • Serves 8 •
Per Serving 515 calories, 35g fat (of which 14g saturates), 13g carbohydrate, 1.3g salt • Easy

1.1kg (2½lb) braising steak
3 tbsp olive oil, plus extra to drizzle
16 whole shallots or button onions
225g (8oz) piece chorizo sausage,
    roughly chopped
1 red chilli, seeded and chopped
    (see page 30)
3 bay leaves
3 garlic cloves, crushed
2 tbsp plain flour
2 tbsp smoked paprika
700g jar passata
100ml (3½fl oz) hot beef stock
salt and freshly ground black
    pepper
mashed potatoes and green
    vegetables to serve

**FOR THE MINTED SOURED
CREAM**

284ml carton soured cream
1 tbsp finely chopped fresh mint
1 tbsp extra virgin olive oil, plus
    extra to drizzle

1. Mix together all the ingredients
for the minted soured cream and
season with a little salt and plenty
of coarsely ground black pepper.
Cover and chill in the fridge until
needed.

2. Preheat the oven to 170°C
(150°C fan oven) mark 3. Cut the
braising steak into large cubes,
slightly larger than bite-size.

3. Heat the oil in a 4 litre (7 pint)
flameproof casserole until really
hot. Brown the beef, a few cubes
at a time, over a high heat until it is
deep brown all over. Remove with
a slotted spoon and put to one
side. Repeat with the remaining
beef until all the pieces have
been browned.

4. Reduce the heat under the
casserole, then add the shallots or
button onions, the chorizo, chilli,
bay leaves and garlic. Fry for
7–10 minutes until the shallots are
golden brown and beginning to
soften. Put the meat back into the
casserole and stir in the flour
and paprika. Cook, stirring, for
1–2 minutes, then add the passata
and season.

5. Cover and cook in the oven
for 2½ hours or until the beef is
meltingly tender. Check halfway
through cooking – if the beef looks
dry, add the hot stock. Serve with
the minted soured cream, drizzled
with a little olive oil and a grinding
of black pepper, and some creamy
mashed potatoes and green
vegetables.

GET AHEAD
*Complete the recipe, cool and chill
up to three days ahead, or freeze for
up to one month. To use, if frozen,
thaw overnight at a cool room
temperature. Put the goulash back
into the casserole, bring to the boil,
reduce the heat and simmer gently
for 15–20 minutes until piping hot,
adding 100ml (3½fl oz) hot beef
stock if it looks dry.*

Roast Rib of Beef

Preparation Time 5 minutes • Cooking Time about 2¾ hours, plus resting • Serves 8 •
Per Serving 807 calories, 53g fat (of which 24g saturates), 2g carbohydrate, 0.5g salt • Easy

**2-bone rib of beef (weight about
    2.5–2.7kg/5½ –6lb)**
1 tbsp plain flour
1 tbsp English mustard powder
150ml (¼ pint) red wine
600ml (1 pint) beef stock
**salt and freshly ground black
    pepper**
fresh thyme sprigs to garnish
**Yorkshire puddings, roasted root
    vegetables and a green vegetable
    to serve**

1. Preheat the oven to 230°C (210°C fan oven) mark 8. Put the beef, fat side up, in a roasting tin just large enough to hold the joint. Mix the flour and mustard together in a small bowl and season with salt and ground black pepper, then rub the mixture over the beef. Roast in the centre of the oven for 30 minutes.

2. Move the beef to a lower shelf, near the bottom of the oven. Reduce the oven temperature to 220°C (200°C fan oven) mark 7 and continue to roast the beef for a further 2 hours, basting occasionally.

3. Transfer the beef to a carving dish, cover loosely with foil and leave to rest while you make the gravy. Skim off most of the fat from the roasting tin. Put the roasting tin on the hob over a high heat, pour in the wine and boil vigorously until very syrupy. Pour in the stock, bring to the boil and, again, boil until syrupy. Add 600ml (1 pint) vegetable water and boil until syrupy. There should be about 450ml (¾ pint) gravy. Taste and adjust the seasoning.

4. Remove the rib bone and carve the beef. Garnish with thyme and serve with the gravy, Yorkshire puddings and roasted vegetables.

COOK'S TIP
Buy the best quality meat you can afford. The beef should be a dark red colour, not bright red, and have a good marbling of fat.

Perfect Cold Roast Beef

Preparation Time 15 minutes, plus overnight chilling • Cooking Time about 2 hours • Serves 8 •
Per Serving 322 calories, 8g fat (of which 3g saturates), 4g carbohydrate, 0.5g salt • Easy

**2kg (4½lb) rolled topside beef
 roasting joint**
2 tbsp light brown soft sugar
1 tbsp English mustard powder
1 tbsp vegetable oil
**coleslaw, watercress leaves and
 creamed horseradish to serve**

1. Take the beef out of the fridge 1 hour before cooking to allow it to come up to room temperature.

2. Preheat the oven to 200°C (180°C fan oven) mark 6. Pat the beef dry with kitchen paper and take a note of its weight (just in case). Mix the sugar and mustard powder in a small bowl and rub over the beef. Heat the oil in a large frying pan over a high heat and fry the beef on all sides, until well browned.

3. Sit the beef in a roasting tin just large enough to hold the joint and cover loosely with foil. Roast in the oven for 15 minutes per 500g (1lb 2oz) for rare meat, 20 minutes per 500g (1lb 2oz) for medium-rare meat or 25 minutes per 500g (1lb 2oz) for well-done meat, then roast for an extra 10 minutes on top of the calculated time. Or use a meat thermometer – for medium-rare meat the internal temperature of the beef should be 60°C.

4. Transfer the beef to a board and leave to cool completely. Wrap well in foil and chill overnight. (You can also serve this beef hot as part of a Sunday lunch – just leave it to rest for 30 minutes after roasting, then carve.)

5. An hour before serving, slice the beef thinly and arrange on a serving plate, then cover. Serve with coleslaw, watercress leaves and creamed horseradish.

GET AHEAD
Cook the beef to the end of step 3 up to 3 days ahead, then complete the recipe and chill.

Steak & Onion Puff Pie

Preparation Time 30 minutes • Cooking Time about 2½ hours • Serves 4 •
Per Serving 1036 calories, 67g fat (of which 10g saturates), 65g carbohydrate, 1.4g salt • Easy

3 tbsp vegetable oil
2 onions, sliced
900g (2lb) casserole beef, cut into
chunks
3 tbsp plain flour, plus extra to dust
500ml (17fl oz) hot beef stock
2 fresh rosemary sprigs, bruised
500g pack puff pastry
1 medium egg, beaten, to glaze
salt and freshly ground black
pepper

1. Preheat the oven to 170°C
(150°C fan oven) mark 3.

2. Heat 1 tbsp of the oil in a large
flameproof casserole. Add the
onions and sauté for 10 minutes or
until golden. Lift out and put to one
side. Sear the meat in the same
casserole, in batches, using more
oil as necessary, until brown all
over. Lift out each batch as soon as
it is browned and put to one side.
Add the flour to the casserole and
cook for 1–2 minutes to brown. Put
the onions and beef back into the
casserole, add the hot stock and
the rosemary and season well with
salt and ground black pepper.
Cover and bring to the boil, then
cook in the oven for 1½ hours or
until the meat is tender.

3. About 30 minutes before the end
of the cooking time, lightly dust a
worksurface with flour and roll out
the pastry. Using a 1.1 litre (2 pint)
pie dish as a template, cut out a lid,
or use four 300ml (½ pint) dishes
and cut out four lids. Put on a baking
sheet and chill.

4. Take the casserole out of the
oven. Increase the oven temperature
to 220°C (200°C fan oven) mark 7.
Pour the beef mixture into the pie
dish (or dishes), brush the edge
with water and put on the pastry lid.
Press lightly to seal. Lightly score the
top and brush with the egg. Put the
dish back on the baking sheet and
bake for 30 minutes or until the
pastry is risen and golden. Serve
immediately.

FREEZING TIP
To freeze Complete the recipe to
the end of step 3. Cool the casserole
quickly. Put the beef mixture into a
pie dish. Brush the dish edge with
water, put on the pastry and press
down lightly to seal. Score the pastry.
Cover with clingfilm and freeze for
up to three months.
To use Thaw overnight at cool room
temperature or in the fridge. Lightly
score the pastry, brush with beaten
egg and cook in an oven preheated
to 220°C (200°C fan oven) mark 7
for 35 minutes or until the pastry is
brown and the filling piping hot.

Braised Oxtail

Preparation Time 20 minutes • Cooking Time about 4½ hours • Serves 6 •
Per Serving 616 calories, 35g fat (of which 12g saturates), 16g carbohydrate, 1.2g salt • Easy

**2 oxtails (total weight about
1.6kg/3½lb), trimmed**
2 tbsp plain flour
4 tbsp oil
2 large onions, sliced
900ml (1½ pints) beef stock
150ml (¼ pint) red wine
1 tbsp tomato purée
finely grated zest of ½ lemon
2 bay leaves
2 medium carrots, chopped
450g (1lb) parsnips, chopped
**salt and freshly ground black
pepper**
**freshly chopped flat-leafed parsley
to garnish**

1. Cut the oxtails into large pieces. Put the flour into a plastic bag, season with salt and ground black pepper, then toss the meat in it. Heat the oil in a large flameproof casserole and brown the oxtail pieces, a few at a time. Remove from the casserole with a slotted spoon and put to one side.

2. Add the onions to the casserole and fry over a medium heat for about 10 minutes until softened and lightly browned. Stir in any remaining flour.

3. Stir in the stock, red wine, tomato purée, lemon zest and bay leaves and season with salt and ground black pepper. Bring to the boil, then put the oxtail back into the casserole and reduce the heat. Cover and simmer very gently for 2 hours.

4. Skim off the fat from the surface, then stir in the carrots and parsnips. Re-cover the casserole and simmer very gently for a further 2 hours or until the oxtail is very tender.

5. Skim off all the fat from the surface, then check the seasoning. Serve scattered with chopped parsley.

Luxury Lamb & Leek Hotpot

Preparation Time 20 minutes • Cooking Time 2 hours 50 minutes • Serves 6 • Per Serving 530 calories, 33g fat (of which 20g saturates), 27g carbohydrate, 0.5g salt • Easy

50g (2oz) butter

400g (14oz) leeks, trimmed and sliced

1 medium onion, chopped

1 tbsp olive oil

800g (1¾lb) casserole lamb, cubed and tossed with 1 tbsp plain flour

2 garlic cloves, crushed

800g (1¾lb) waxy potatoes, such as Desirée, sliced

3 tbsp freshly chopped flat-leafed parsley

1 tsp freshly chopped thyme

300ml (½ pint) lamb stock

142ml carton double cream

salt and ground black pepper

1. Melt half the butter in a 3.5 litre (6¼ pint) flameproof casserole. Add the leeks and onion, stir to coat, then cover and cook over a low heat for 10 minutes.

2. Transfer the leeks and onion on to a large sheet of greaseproof paper. Add the oil to the casserole and heat, then brown the meat in batches with the garlic and plenty of seasoning. Remove and put to one side on another large sheet of greaseproof paper.

3. Preheat the oven to 170°C (150°C fan oven) mark 3. Put half the potatoes in a layer over the bottom of the casserole and season. Add the meat, then spoon the leek mixture on top. Arrange a layer of overlapping potatoes on top of that, sprinkle with herbs, then pour in the stock.

4. Bring the casserole to the boil, then cover and transfer to a low shelf in the oven and cook for about 1 hour 50 minutes. Remove from the oven, dot with the remaining butter and add the cream. Return to the oven and cook, uncovered, for 30–40 minutes until the potatoes are golden brown.

Braised Lamb Shanks with Cannellini Beans

Preparation Time 15 minutes • Cooking Time 3 hours • Serves 6 • Per Serving 382 calories, 18g fat (of which 6g saturates), 29g carbohydrate, 1.2g salt • Gluten Free • Dairy Free • Easy

3 tbsp olive oil
6 lamb shanks
1 large onion, chopped
3 carrots, sliced
3 celery sticks, sliced
2 garlic cloves, crushed
2 × 400g cans chopped tomatoes
125ml (4fl oz) balsamic vinegar
2 bay leaves
2 × 400g cans cannellini beans,
    drained and rinsed
salt and ground black pepper

1. Preheat the oven to 170°C (150°C fan oven) mark 3. Heat the oil in a large flameproof casserole and brown the lamb shanks, in two batches, all over. Remove and set aside.

2. Add the onion, carrots, celery and garlic to the casserole and cook gently until softened and just beginning to colour.

3. Return the lamb to the casserole and add the chopped tomatoes and balsamic vinegar, giving the mixture a good stir. Season with salt and pepper and add the bay leaves. Bring to a simmer, cover and cook on the hob for 5 minutes.

4. Transfer to the oven and cook for 1½–2 hours or until the lamb shanks are nearly tender.

5. Remove the casserole from the oven and add the cannellini beans. Cover and return to the oven for a further 30 minutes, then serve.

Italian Braised Leg of Lamb

Preparation Time 15 minutes • Cooking Time about 5 hours • Serves 6 • Per Serving 400 calories,
18g fat (of which 6g saturates), 17g carbohydrate, 0.7g salt • Gluten Free • Dairy Free • Easy

2.3kg (5lb) boned leg of lamb
50ml (2fl oz) olive oil
700g (1½lb) onions, roughly chopped
1 each red, orange and yellow peppers, seeded and roughly chopped
2 red chillies, seeded and finely chopped (see page 30)

1 garlic bulb, cloves separated and peeled
3 tbsp dried oregano
750ml bottle dry white wine
3 × 400g cans cherry tomatoes
salt and ground black pepper

1. Preheat the oven to 170°C (150°C fan oven) mark 3. Season the lamb with salt and pepper. Heat 2 tbsp oil in a large deep flameproof casserole and brown the meat well. Remove and set aside. Wipe the pan clean.

2. Heat the remaining oil in the casserole and fry the onions, peppers, chillies, garlic and oregano over a medium heat for 10–15 minutes until the onions are translucent and golden brown. Stir in the wine and tomatoes and bring to the boil. Bubble for 10 minutes.

3. Put the lamb on top of the vegetables and season. Baste the meat with the sauce and cover the casserole tightly with foil and a lid. Cook in the oven for 4 hours, basting occasionally.

4. Uncover and cook for a further 30 minutes. Serve the lamb carved into thick slices with the sauce spooned over.

Lamb & Pasta Pot

Preparation Time 10 minutes • Cooking Time 50 minutes • Serves 4 • Per Serving 686 calories,
36g fat (of which 16g saturates), 18g carbohydrate, 1.4g salt • Dairy Free • Easy

**1 half leg of lamb roasting joint,
  about 1.1kg (2½lb)**
**125g (4oz) smoked streaky bacon,
  chopped**
150ml (¼ pint) red wine
**400g can chopped tomatoes with
  chilli, or 400g (14oz) passata**
75g (3oz) dried pasta shapes
12 sunblush tomatoes
**150g (5oz) chargrilled artichokes in
  oil, drained and halved**
basil leaves to garnish

1. Preheat the oven to 200°C
(180°C fan oven) mark 6. Put the
lamb and bacon into a small deep
flameproof roasting tin and fry for
5 minutes or until the lamb is brown
all over and the bacon is beginning
to crisp.

2. Remove the lamb and set aside.
Pour the wine into the tin with the
bacon – it should bubble at once.
Stir well, scraping the base to loosen
any crusty bits, then leave to bubble
until half the wine has evaporated.
Stir in 300ml (½ pint) water and add
the chopped tomatoes or passata,
pasta and sunblush tomatoes.

3. Put the lamb on a rack over the
roasting tin so that the juices drip
into the pasta. Cook, uncovered, in
the oven for about 35 minutes.

4. Stir the artichokes into the pasta
and put everything back in the oven
for 5 minutes or until the lamb is
tender and the pasta cooked. Slice
the lamb thickly. Serve with the
pasta and scatter the basil on top.

Turkish Lamb Stew

Preparation Time 10 minutes • Cooking Time 1½–2 hours • Serves 4 • Per Serving 389 calories, 20g fat (of which 7g saturates), 28g carbohydrate, 1.2g salt • Gluten Free • Dairy Free • Easy

2 tbsp olive oil

400g (14oz) lean lamb fillet, cubed

1 red onion, sliced

1 garlic clove, crushed

1 potato, quartered

400g can chopped plum tomatoes

1 red pepper, seeded and sliced

200g (7oz) canned chickpeas, drained and rinsed

1 aubergine, cut into chunks

200ml (7fl oz) lamb stock

1 tbsp red wine vinegar

1 tsp each freshly chopped thyme, rosemary and oregano

8 black olives, halved and pitted

salt and ground black pepper

1. Heat 1 tbsp oil in a flameproof casserole and brown the lamb over a high heat. Reduce the heat and add the remaining oil, the onion and garlic, then cook until soft.

2. Preheat the oven to 170°C (150°C fan oven) mark 3. Add the potato, tomatoes, red pepper, chickpeas, aubergine, stock, vinegar and herbs to the pan. Season, stir and bring to the boil. Cover the pan, transfer to the oven and cook for 1–1½ hours until the lamb is tender.

3. About 15 minutes before the end of the cooking time, add the olives.

Lamb, Potato & Peanut Curry

Preparation Time 20 minutes • Cooking Time about 2 hours • Serves 8 • Per Serving 664 calories,
47g fat (of which 20g saturates), 19g carbohydrate, 0.5g salt • Gluten Free • Dairy Free • Easy

2 tbsp olive oil
1 medium onion, chopped
1 tbsp peeled and grated fresh
   root ginger
1.6kg (3½lb) leg of lamb, diced
3–4 tbsp Massaman paste (see
   Cook's Tip)
1 tbsp fish sauce
2 tbsp peanut butter
100g (3½oz) ground almonds
400ml can coconut milk

600ml (1 pint) hot chicken stock
1–2 tbsp dry sherry
500g (1lb 2oz) small potatoes,
   quartered
200g (7oz) green beans, trimmed
75g (3oz) toasted peanuts, roughly
   chopped, to garnish
20g pack coriander, finely
   chopped, to garnish
2 limes, quartered, and rice
   (optional) to serve

1. Preheat the oven to 170°C (150°C fan oven) mark 3. Heat the oil in a large flameproof casserole. Add the onion and cook over a medium heat for 7–8 minutes until golden. Add the ginger and cook for 1 minute. Spoon the onion mixture out of the pan and set aside. Add the lamb and fry in batches until browned. Set aside.

2. Add the Massaman paste, fish sauce and peanut butter to the casserole dish and fry for 2–3 minutes, then add the reserved onion and ginger mixture and lamb pieces, the ground almonds, coconut milk, hot stock and sherry.

3. Bring to the boil, then cover with a lid and cook in the oven for 1 hour. Add the potatoes and cook for a further 40 minutes, uncovered, adding the green beans for the last 20 minutes. Garnish the curry with toasted peanuts and coriander. Serve with freshly cooked rice, if you like, and lime wedges to squeeze over the curry.

COOK'S TIP

Massaman paste is a Thai curry paste. The ingredients include red chillies, roasted shallots, roasted garlic, galangal, lemongrass, roasted coriander seeds, roasted cumin, roasted cloves, white pepper, salt and shrimp paste. It's available in supermarkets or Asian food stores.

Braised Lamb Shanks

Preparation Time 20–25 minutes • Cooking Time 2¾ hours • Serves 6 • Per Serving 355 calories, 16g fat (of which 6g saturates), 23g carbohydrate, 1.2g salt • Gluten Free • Dairy Free • Easy

6 small lamb shanks
450g (1lb) shallots, peeled but left whole
2 medium aubergines, cut into small dice
2 tbsp olive oil
3 tbsp harissa paste
pared zest of 1 orange and juice of 3 large oranges
200ml (7fl oz) medium sherry

700g (1½lb) passata
300ml (½ pint) hot vegetable or lamb stock
75g (3oz) ready-to-eat dried apricots
75g (3oz) cherries (optional)
a large pinch of saffron threads
couscous and French beans (optional) to serve

1. Preheat the oven to 170°C (150°C fan oven) mark 3. Heat a large flameproof casserole over a medium heat and brown the lamb shanks all over. Allow 10–12 minutes to do this – the better the colour now, the better the flavour of the finished dish.

2. Remove the lamb and put to one side. Add the shallots, aubergines and oil to the casserole and cook over a high heat, stirring from time to time, until the shallots and aubergines are golden and beginning to soften.

3. Reduce the heat and add the lamb and all the other ingredients except the couscous and beans. The liquid should come halfway up the shanks. Bring to the boil, then cover tightly and put into the oven for 2½ hours. Test the lamb with a fork – it should be so tender that it almost falls off the bone.

4. If the cooking liquid looks too thin, remove the lamb to a heated serving plate, then bubble the sauce on the hob until reduced and thickened. Put the lamb back into the casserole. Serve with couscous and French beans, if you like.

COOK'S TIP
Cooking lamb shanks in a rich sauce in the oven at a low temperature makes the meat meltingly tender.

Lamb, Prune & Almond Tagine

Preparation Time 20 minutes, plus marinating • Cooking Time 2½ hours • Serves 6 • Per Serving 652 calories, 44g fat (of which 16g saturates), 31g carbohydrate, 0.6g salt • Gluten Free • Easy

2 tsp coriander seeds

2 tsp cumin seeds

2 tsp chilli powder

1 tbsp paprika

1 tbsp ground turmeric

5 garlic cloves, chopped

6 tbsp olive oil

1.4kg (3lb) lamb leg steaks

75g (3oz) ghee or clarified butter (see Cook's Tip)

2 large onions, finely chopped

1 carrot, roughly chopped

900ml (1½ pints) lamb stock

300g (11oz) ready-to-eat prunes

4 cinnamon sticks

4 bay leaves

50g (2oz) ground almonds

12 shallots

1 tbsp honey

salt and ground black pepper

toasted blanched almonds and freshly chopped flat-leafed parsley to garnish

couscous to serve

1. Using a pestle and mortar or a blender, combine the coriander and cumin seeds, chilli powder, paprika, turmeric, garlic and 4 tbsp oil. Coat the lamb with the paste, then cover and chill for at least 5 hours.

2. Preheat the oven to 170°C (150°C fan oven) mark 3. Melt 25g (1oz) ghee or butter in a large flameproof casserole. Add the onions and carrot and cook until soft. Remove and put to one side. Fry the paste-coated lamb on both sides in the remaining ghee or butter. Add a little of the stock and bring to the boil, scraping up the sediment from the bottom. Put the onions and carrot back in the casserole and add 100g (3½oz) prunes. Add the remaining stock with the cinnamon sticks, bay leaves and ground almonds. Season, then cover and cook in the oven for 2 hours or until the meat is really tender.

3. Meanwhile, fry the shallots in the remaining oil and the honey until they turn a deep golden brown. Add to the casserole 30–40 minutes before the end of the cooking time.

4. Take the lamb out of the sauce and put to one side. Bring the sauce to the boil, then reduce to a thick consistency. Put the lamb back in the casserole, add the remaining prunes and bubble for 3–4 minutes. Garnish with the almonds and parsley. Serve hot with couscous.

COOK'S TIP

To make clarified butter, heat butter in a pan without allowing it to colour. Skim off the foam; the solids will sink. Pour the clear butter into a bowl through a lined sieve. Leave for 10 minutes. Pour into a bowl, leaving any sediment behind. Cool. Store in a jar in the fridge for up to six months.

Moroccan Lamb Stew

Preparation Time 20 minutes • Cooking Time about 1 hour 20 minutes • Serves 6 • Per Serving 274 calories, 11g fat (of which 5g saturates), 25g carbohydrate, 0.2g salt • Dairy Free • Easy

500g (1lb 2oz) lamb shoulder, well trimmed to remove excess fat, then roughly cubed
15g (½oz) plain flour
½ tbsp sunflower oil
1 onion, thickly sliced
2 carrots, roughly chopped
2 garlic cloves, crushed
2 tsp harissa paste

1 tsp ground cinnamon
2 × 400g cans chopped tomatoes
75g (3oz) dried apricots, roughly chopped
100g (3½oz) couscous
a large handful of curly parsley, roughly chopped
salt and ground black pepper

1. Dust the lamb with the flour. Heat the oil in a large pan and brown the lamb in batches. Set aside. In the same pan, add the onions and carrots and gently fry for 10 minutes. Add a splash of water if they start to stick to the pan.

2. Stir in the garlic, harissa and cinnamon and cook for 1 minute. Add a splash of water and use a wooden spoon to help scrape any goodness from the bottom of the pan, then stir it in. Pour in the tomatoes and return the lamb to the pan. Stir in the apricots and season. Cover and simmer for 1 hour or until the lamb is tender. Season to taste.

3. Meanwhile, put the couscous into a bowl and add boiling water according to the pack instructions. Cover with clingfilm and leave for 10 minutes. When ready, fluff up the grains with a fork, then stir in the parsley. Season. Serve the lamb topped with spoonfuls of couscous (see Cook's Tip).

COOK'S TIP

Watching your carb intake? Serving the couscous as a garnish on the stew rather than as a substantial side dish is a satisfying alternative.

Lamb & Bamboo Shoot Red Curry

Preparation Time 10 minutes • Cooking Time 45 minutes • Serves 4 • Per Serving 397 calories,
25g fat (of which 8g saturates), 17g carbohydrate, 0.4g salt • Gluten Free • Dairy Free • Easy

2 tbsp sunflower oil

1 large onion, cut into wedges

2 garlic cloves, finely chopped

450g (1lb) lean boneless lamb, cut
into 3cm (1¼in) cubes

2 tbsp Thai red curry paste

150ml (¼ pint) lamb or beef stock

2 tbsp Thai fish sauce

2 tsp soft brown sugar

200g can bamboo shoots, drained
and thinly sliced

1 red pepper, seeded and thinly
sliced

2 tbsp freshly chopped mint

1 tbsp freshly chopped basil

25g (1oz) unsalted peanuts, toasted
rice to serve

1. Heat the oil in a wok or large frying pan, add the onion and garlic and fry over a medium heat for 5 minutes.

2. Add the lamb and the curry paste and stir-fry for 5 minutes. Add the stock, fish sauce and sugar and bring to the boil, then reduce the heat, cover the pan and simmer gently for 20 minutes.

3. Stir the bamboo shoots, red pepper and herbs into the curry and cook, uncovered, for a further 10 minutes. Stir in the peanuts and serve immediately, with rice.

Lamb & Orzo Stew

Preparation Time 10 minutes • Cooking Time about 2 hours • Serves 6 •
Per Serving 490 calories, 22g fat (of which 9g saturates), 32g carbohydrate, 0.8g salt • Easy

1 tbsp vegetable oil

1kg (2¼lb) diced lamb (leg or
    shoulder), excess fat trimmed

2 red onions, finely sliced

1 tbsp dried oregano

1 tsp ground cinnamon

400g can chopped tomatoes

1.2 litres (2¼ pints) vegetable stock

200g (7oz) orzo pasta

50g (2oz) pitted black olives,
    roughly chopped

a large handful of fresh parsley,
    roughly chopped

salt and freshly ground black
    pepper

1. Heat the oil in a large heatproof casserole dish or pan and brown the lamb in batches. Once all the meat is browned, lift out and put to one side on a plate.

2. Put the casserole/pan back onto the heat, add the onions and cook gently for 10 minutes or until softened (add a little water if the pan looks too dry). Stir in the oregano and cinnamon and cook for 1 minute, then stir in the tomatoes, stock and lamb. Cover and simmer for 1¼ hours, stirring occasionally, or until the lamb is tender.

3. Stir the orzo into the casserole or pan and cook, uncovered, for a further 10–12 minutes until the orzo is tender. (Once the orzo is tender, it will continue to swell on standing. If you're not serving it immediately, add a little extra water until the desired consistency is reached.) Next, stir in the olives and most of the parsley. Check the seasoning and garnish with the remaining parsley. Serve immediately.

FREEZING TIP

To freeze Complete the recipe to the end of step 2, then leave to cool completely. Transfer the mixture to a freezerproof container, cover and freeze for up to three months.

To use Thaw overnight in the fridge. Reheat gently in a large pan and complete the recipe to serve.

Lamb & Barley Stew

Preparation Time 15 minutes • Cooking Time 2½ hours • Serves 6 • Per Serving 536 calories, 28g fat (of which 12g saturates), 14g carbohydrate, 1.2g salt • Easy

2 tbsp plain wholemeal flour

1.4kg (3lb) boned leg or shoulder of lamb, trimmed of fat and cubed

3 streaky bacon rashers, rind removed

25g (1oz) butter

2 medium onions, chopped

2 medium carrots, sliced

125g (4oz) turnip or swede, diced

2 celery sticks, diced

2 tbsp pearl barley

2 tsp mixed freshly chopped herbs, such as thyme, rosemary, parsley, basil

300ml (½ pint) lamb or beef stock

salt and freshly ground black pepper

freshly chopped flat-leafed parsley to garnish

1. Season the flour with salt and ground black pepper, then toss the lamb in the flour.

2. Dry-fry the bacon in a large flameproof casserole until the fat runs. Add the butter and lamb and fry until browned all over, stirring. Using a slotted spoon, remove the lamb and bacon from the casserole and put to one side.

3. Add the onions, carrots, turnip or swede and the celery to the casserole and fry for 5–10 minutes until beginning to brown.

4. Put the lamb back into the casserole, add the pearl barley and herbs and pour in the stock. Bring to the boil, then reduce the heat, cover and simmer for 2 hours, stirring occasionally to prevent sticking, or until the lamb is tender.

5. Serve hot, sprinkled with parsley.

Irish Stew

Preparation Time 15 minutes • Cooking Time about 2¼ hours • Serves 4 • Per Serving 419 calories,
20g fat (of which 9g saturates), 24g carbohydrate, 0.6g salt • Easy

**700g (1½lb) middle neck lamb
cutlets, fat trimmed**
2 onions, thinly sliced
450g (1lb) potatoes, thinly sliced
**1 tbsp freshly chopped flat-leafed
parsley, plus extra to garnish**
1 tbsp dried thyme
300ml (½ pint) hot lamb stock
**salt and freshly ground black
pepper**

1. Preheat the oven to 170°C
(150°C fan oven) mark 3. Layer
the meat, onions and potatoes in
a deep casserole dish, sprinkling
some herbs and salt and ground
black pepper between each layer.
Finish with a layer of potato,
overlapping the slices neatly.

2. Pour the hot stock over the
potatoes, then cover with
greaseproof paper and a lid. Cook
in the oven for about 2 hours until
the meat is tender.

3. Preheat the grill. Take the lid
off the casserole and remove the
paper. Put under the grill and
brown the top of the potatoes.
Sprinkle with chopped parsley
and serve immediately.

Warming Winter Casserole

Preparation Time 20 minutes • Cooking Time 1 hour • Serves 4 • Per Serving 407 calories, 16g fat (of which 3g saturates), 32g carbohydrate, 1g salt • Gluten Free • Dairy Free • Easy

2 tbsp olive oil
500g (1lb 2oz) pork fillet, cubed
1 onion, finely chopped
2 garlic cloves, finely chopped
1 tsp ground cinnamon
1 tbsp ground coriander
1 tsp ground cumin
2.5cm (1in) piece fresh root ginger, peeled and grated
400g can mixed beans or chickpeas, drained

1 red pepper, seeded and sliced
50g (2oz) ready-to-eat dried apricots, roughly chopped
300ml (½ pint) chicken stock
25g (1oz) flaked almonds, toasted
salt and ground black pepper
freshly chopped flat-leafed parsley to garnish
brown basmati rice to serve

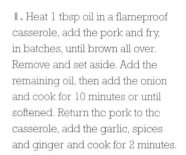

1. Heat 1 tbsp oil in a flameproof casserole, add the pork and fry, in batches, until brown all over. Remove and set aside. Add the remaining oil, then add the onion and cook for 10 minutes or until softened. Return the pork to the casserole, add the garlic, spices and ginger and cook for 2 minutes.

2. Add the mixed beans, red pepper, apricots and stock. Season well with salt and pepper, then stir and bring to the boil. Reduce the heat to the lowest setting and simmer, covered, for 40 minutes, adding a little extra stock if it begins to look dry.

3. Check the seasoning and sprinkle with the almonds, then garnish with the parsley and serve with brown basmati rice.

TRY SOMETHING DIFFERENT
Instead of pork, use the same quantity of lean lamb, such as leg, trimmed of excess fat and cut into cubes.

Cumberland Glazed Baked Gammon

Preparation Time 30 minutes • Cooking Time about 4¼ hours • Serves 16 •
Per Serving 406 calories, 21g fat (of which 7g saturates), 4g carbohydrate, 6.3g salt • Easy

**4.5kg (10lb) smoked gammon joint,
on the bone**
2 celery sticks, roughly chopped
1 onion, quartered
1 carrot, roughly chopped
1 tsp black peppercorns
1 tbsp cloves
75g (3oz) redcurrant sprigs

**FOR THE CUMBERLAND
GLAZE**
**grated zest and juice of ½ lemon
and ½ orange**
4 tbsp redcurrant jelly
1 tsp Dijon mustard
2 tbsp port
**salt and freshly ground black
pepper**

1. Put the gammon into a large pan. Add the celery, onion, carrot and peppercorns. Cover the meat and vegetables with cold water and bring to the boil, then cover, reduce the heat and simmer for 2¾–3½ hours or allowing 15–20 minutes per 450g (1lb) plus 15 minutes. Lift the gammon out of the pan. Preheat the oven to 200°C (180°C fan oven) mark 6.

2. Meanwhile, make the glaze. Heat the lemon and orange zests and juices, redcurrant jelly, mustard and port in a pan to dissolve the jelly. Bring to the boil and bubble for 5 minutes or until syrupy. Season with salt and ground black pepper to taste.

3. Remove the gammon rind and score the fat in a diamond pattern. Put the gammon into a roasting tin, then stud the fat with the cloves. Spoon the glaze evenly over the gammon joint.

4. Roast the gammon for 40 minutes, basting the meat with any juices. Add the redcurrant sprigs 10 minutes before the end of the cooking time. Serve the gammon hot or cold, carved into thin slices, with the redcurrant sprigs.

One-pot Gammon Stew

Preparation Time 15 minutes • Cooking Time 1 hour 10 minutes • Serves 4 • Per Serving 680 calories, 30g fat (of which 11g saturates), 41g carbohydrate, 6.3g salt • Gluten Free • Easy

1 tbsp olive oil

1.1kg (2½lb) smoked gammon joint

8 shallots, blanched in boiling water, drained, peeled and chopped into chunks

3 carrots, chopped into chunks

3 celery sticks, chopped into chunks

4 large Desirée potatoes, unpeeled

450ml (¾ pint) each apple juice and hot vegetable stock

½ small Savoy cabbage

25g (1oz) butter

1. Preheat the oven to 190°C (170°C fan oven) mark 5. Heat the oil in a large flameproof casserole. Add the gammon and cook for 5 minutes or until brown all over. Remove from the pan.

2. Add the shallots, carrots and celery to the pan and fry for 3–4 minutes until starting to soften.

3. Return the gammon to the pan. Chop the potatoes into quarters and add to the pan with the apple juice and hot stock. Cover and bring to the boil, then transfer to the oven and cook for 50 minutes or until the meat is cooked through and the vegetables are tender.

4. Remove from the oven and put the dish back on the hob over a low heat. Shred the cabbage and stir into the pan. Simmer for 2–3 minutes, then stir in the butter and serve.

Ginger & Honey Glazed Ham

Preparation Time about 30 minutes • Cooking Time 5¾ hours • Serves 8–10 • Per Serving 440–550 calories, 15–19g fat (of which 5–6g saturates), 38–48g carbohydrate, 4.4–5.5g salt • Easy

4.5–6.8kg (10–15lb) unsmoked gammon on the bone

2 shallots, halved

6 cloves

3 bay leaves

2 celery sticks, cut into 5cm (2in) pieces

2 tbsp prepared English mustard

5cm (2in) piece fresh root ginger, peeled and thinly sliced

FOR THE GLAZE

225g (8oz) dark brown sugar

2 tbsp runny honey

8 tbsp brandy or Madeira

FOR THE CHUTNEY

4 mangoes, peeled, sliced and chopped into 5cm (2in) chunks

1 tsp mixed spice

4 cardamom pods, seeds removed and crushed

½ tsp ground cinnamon

4 tbsp raisins

1. Put the gammon into a large pan. Add the shallots, cloves, bay leaves and celery and enough cold water to cover. Bring to the boil, then cover, reduce the heat and simmer gently for about 5 hours. Remove any scum with a slotted spoon. Lift the ham out of the pan, discard the vegetables and herbs and leave to cool.

2. Preheat the oven to 200°C (180°C fan oven) mark 6. Using a sharp knife, carefully cut away the ham's thick skin to leave an even layer of fat. Score a diamond pattern in the fat and put the ham into a roasting tin. Smother evenly with the mustard and tuck the ginger into the scored fat.

3. To make the glaze, put the sugar, honey and brandy or Madeira into a pan and heat until the sugar has dissolved. Brush over the ham.

4. Mix all the chutney ingredients in a bowl, add any remaining glaze, then spoon around the ham.

5. Cook the ham for 30–40 minutes, basting every 10 minutes. Remove the ham from the roasting tin and put to one side. Stir the chutney and put it under the grill for 5 minutes to allow the mango to caramelise. Transfer the chutney to a side dish and serve with the ham.

Honey Pork with Roast Potatoes & Apples

Preparation Time 20 minutes • Cooking Time 1 hour 40 minutes, plus resting • Serves 4 • Per Serving 830 calories, 55g fat (of which 19g saturates), 40g carbohydrate, 0.4g salt • Gluten Free • Easy

- **1kg (2¼lb) loin of pork, with skin and four bones**
- **4 tbsp olive oil**
- **25g (1oz) butter**
- **700g (1¼lb) Charlotte potatoes, scrubbed and halved**
- **1 large onion, cut into eight wedges**
- **1 tbsp clear honey mixed with 1 tbsp wholegrain mustard**
- **2 Cox's Orange Pippin apples, cored and each cut into six wedges**
- **12 fresh sage leaves**
- **175ml (6fl oz) dry cider**
- **salt and ground black pepper**

1. Preheat the oven to 240°C (220°C fan oven) mark 9. Put the pork on a board and use a paring knife to score the skin into thin strips, cutting about halfway into the fat underneath. Rub 1 tsp salt and 2 tbsp oil over the skin and season well with pepper. Put the meat on a rack, skin side up, over a large roasting tin (or just put the pork into the tin)

2. Roast for 25 minutes. Turn the oven down to 190°C (170°C fan oven) mark 5 and continue to roast for 15 minutes. Add the remaining oil and the butter to the roasting tin. Scatter the potatoes and onion around the meat, season and continue to roast for 45 minutes.

3. Brush the meat with the honey and mustard mixture. Add the apples and sage leaves to the tin and roast for a further 15 minutes or until the pork is cooked.

4. Remove the pork from the tin and wrap completely with foil, then leave to rest for 10 minutes. Put the potatoes, onions and apples into a warmed serving dish and put back in the oven to keep warm.

5. Put the roasting tin on the hob, add the cider and stir well to make a thin gravy. Season.

6. Cut the meat away from the bone. Cut between each bone. Pull the crackling away from the meat and cut into strips. Carve the joint, giving each person some crackling and a bone to chew. Serve with the gravy and potatoes, onion and apples.

Pork & Apple Hotpot

Preparation Time 15 minutes • Cooking Time 2–2¼ hours • Serves 4 • Per Serving 592 calories, 18g fat (of which 7g saturates), 56g carbohydrate, 1g salt • **Easy**

1 tbsp olive oil
900g (2lb) pork shoulder steaks
3 onions, cut into wedges
1 large Bramley apple, peeled, cored and thickly sliced
1 tbsp plain flour
600ml (1 pint) hot weak chicken or vegetable stock
¼ Savoy cabbage, sliced
2 fresh thyme sprigs
900g (2lb) large potatoes, cut into 2cm (¾in) slices
25g (1oz) butter
salt and ground black pepper

1. Preheat the oven to 170°C (150°C fan oven) mark 3. Heat the oil in a large non-stick flameproof and freezerproof casserole until very hot, then fry the steaks, two at a time, for 5 minutes or until golden all over. Remove the steaks from the pan and set aside.

2. In the same casserole, fry the onions for 10 minutes or until soft – add a little water if they start to stick. Stir in the apple and cook for 1 minute, then add the flour to soak up the juices. Gradually add the hot stock and stir until smooth. Season with salt and pepper. Stir in the cabbage and add the pork.

3. Throw in the thyme, overlap the potato slices on top, then dot with the butter. Cover with a tight-fitting lid and cook near the top of the oven for 1 hour. Remove the lid and cook for 30–45 minutes until the potatoes are tender and golden.

COOK'S TIP
Put the hotpot under the grill for 2–3 minutes to crisp up the potatoes, if you like.

FREEZING TIP
To freeze *Cool quickly, then freeze in the casserole for up to three months.*
To use *Thaw overnight at cool room temperature. Preheat the oven to 180°C (160°C fan oven) mark 4. Pour 50ml (2fl oz) hot stock over the hotpot, then cover and reheat for 30 minutes or until piping hot. Uncover and crisp the potatoes under the grill for 2–3 minutes.*

Savoury Pudding

Preparation Time 15 minutes, plus soaking • Cooking Time 1–1¼ hours • Serves 6 • Per Serving 397 calories, 27g fat (of which 15g saturates), 17g carbohydrate, 2.2g salt • Easy

150–175g (5–6oz) thickly sliced white bread (such as sourdough), crusts left on
75g (3oz) butter, softened
Dijon mustard
200g (7oz) sliced ham, very roughly chopped
150g (5oz) mature Cheddar, grated
600ml (1 pint) full-fat milk
5 large eggs, beaten
a pinch of freshly grated nutmeg
2 tbsp freshly chopped herbs, such as parsley, marjoram or thyme
salt and ground black pepper
green salad to serve

1. Spread the bread generously with butter and sparingly with mustard. Put half the slices into the base of a 2 litre (3½ pint) ovenproof dish. Top with the ham and half the cheese, then with the remaining bread, butter side up.

2. Whisk together the milk, eggs, nutmeg and plenty of salt and pepper. Stir in the herbs, then slowly pour the mixture over the bread. Scatter the remaining cheese on top and leave to soak for 15 minutes. Meanwhile, preheat the oven to 180°C (160°C fan oven) mark 4.

3. Put the dish into a roasting tin and fill halfway up the sides with hand-hot water, then cook for 1–1¼ hours until puffed up, golden brown and just set to the centre. Serve immediately, with a green salad.

TRY SOMETHING DIFFERENT
For a vegetarian alternative, leave out the ham and use 250g (9oz) cheese, such as Gruyère. Add three-quarters of the cheese over the first layer of bread and scatter the remaining cheese on top.

Perfect Roast Pork Belly

Preparation Time 15 minutes, plus drying • Cooking Time about 3½ hours, plus resting • Serves 6 •
Per Serving 645 calories, 51g fat (of which 18g saturates), 0g carbohydrate, 0.5g salt • Easy

1.5kg (3lb 2oz) piece pork belly
salt

1. Using a small sharp knife, score lines into the skin (cutting into the fat) about 1cm (½in) apart, but not so deep that you cut into the meat. Pat the pork completely dry, then leave uncovered at room temperature to air dry for about 45 minutes.

2. Preheat the oven to 220°C (200°C fan oven) mark 7. Rub lots of salt over the pork skin. Rest a wire rack in a deep roasting tin and put the pork, skin side up, on the rack. Roast for 30 minutes, then reduce the oven temperature to 170°C (150°C fan oven) mark 3 and continue cooking for 3 hours – by this stage the crackling should be crisp and golden (if not, don't panic, crisp it up under the grill).

3. Transfer the pork to a board and, using a sharp knife, slice off the crackling in one piece (about the outer 2cm/¾in). Cover the pork meat loosely with foil and leave to rest for 30–40 minutes.

4. Cut the crackling into six long strips, then cut the pork belly into six neat squares. Serve each square topped with a strip of crackling.

Spicy Pork & Bean Stew

Preparation Time 15 minutes • Cooking Time 50–55 minutes • Serves 4 • Per Serving 373 calories, 14g fat (of which 3g saturates), 32g carbohydrate, 1.2g salt • Dairy Free • Easy

3 tbsp olive oil

400g (14oz) pork escalopes, cubed

1 red onion, sliced

2 leeks, trimmed and cut into chunks

2 celery sticks, cut into chunks

1 tbsp harissa paste

1 tbsp tomato purée

400g can cherry tomatoes

300ml (½ pint) hot vegetable or chicken stock

400g can cannellini beans, drained and rinsed

1 marinated red pepper, sliced

salt and ground black pepper

freshly chopped flat-leafed parsley to garnish

Greek yogurt and lemon wedges to serve

1. Preheat the oven to 180°C (160°C fan oven) mark 4. Heat 2 tbsp oil in a flameproof casserole and fry the pork in batches until golden. Remove from the pan and set aside.

2. Heat the remaining oil in the pan and fry the onion for 5–10 minutes until softened. Add the leeks and celery and cook for about 5 minutes. Return the pork to the pan and add the harissa and tomato purée. Cook for 1–2 minutes, stirring all the time. Add the tomatoes and hot stock. Season well with salt and pepper. Bring to the boil, then transfer to the oven and cook for 25 minutes.

3. Add the drained beans and red pepper to the mixture and put back into the oven for 5 minutes to warm through. Garnish with parsley and serve with a dollop of Greek yogurt and lemon wedges for squeezing over.

COOK'S TIP

For a simple accompaniment, serve with chunks of crusty baguette or wholegrain bread.

Pork, Garlic & Basil Risotto

Preparation Time 15 minutes • Cooking Time 50 minutes • Serves 6 • Per Serving 431 calories,
18g fat (of which 6g saturates), 28g carbohydrate, 0.7g salt • Easy

6 thin pork escalopes
150g (5oz) Parma ham
about 6 fresh basil leaves
25g (1oz) plain flour
about 75g (3oz) unsalted butter
175g (6oz) onion, finely chopped
2 garlic cloves, crushed
225g (8oz) risotto (arborio) rice
450ml (¾ pint) white wine
450ml (¾ pint) hot chicken stock
3 tbsp fresh ready-made pesto
(see page 16)
50g (2oz) grated Parmesan
4 tbsp freshly chopped flat-leafed
parsley
salt and ground black pepper

1. Preheat the oven to 180°C
(160°C fan oven) mark 4. If needed,
pound the escalopes carefully with
a rolling pin until they are wafer-
thin. Lay a slice of Parma ham on
each escalope and put a basil leaf
on top. Fix in place with a wooden
cocktail stick. Season and dip in the
flour, dusting off any excess.

2. Melt a small knob of the butter
in a deep ovenproof pan and
quickly fry the escalopes in batches
for 2–3 minutes on each side until
lightly golden. Melt a little more
butter for each batch. You will need
about half the butter at this stage.
Remove the escalopes and keep
warm, covered, in the oven.

3. Melt about another 25g (1oz)
butter in the pan and fry the onion
for about 10 minutes or until soft
and golden. Add the garlic and
rice and stir well. Add the wine
and hot stock. Bring to the boil,
then put into the oven and cook,
uncovered, for 20 minutes.

4. Stir in the pesto, Parmesan
and parsley. Push the browned
escalopes into the rice, cover and
put the pan back in the oven for a
further 5 minutes or until the rice
has completely absorbed the liquid
and the escalopes are cooked
through and piping hot.

**TRY SOMETHING
DIFFERENT**
*Use turkey or veal escalopes instead
of pork.*

Great Big Pork Pie

Preparation Time 30 minutes, plus overnight chilling • Cooking Time about 1 hour 20 minutes, plus cooling •
Serves 12 • Per Serving 650 calories, 33g fat (of which 13g saturates), 65g carbohydrate, 1.1g salt • A Little Effort

FOR THE PASTRY
vegetable oil to grease
900g (2lb) plain flour, plus extra
   to dust
1 tsp salt
250g (9oz) lard

FOR THE FILLING
½ tbsp vegetable oil
1 onion, finely chopped
1kg (2¼lb) pork mince
6 smoked streaky bacon rashers,
   cut into 1cm (½in) pieces
¼ tsp mixed spice
a small handful of fresh parsley,
   finely chopped
½ tsp salt
4 tbsp onion marmalade
1 medium egg, beaten
100ml (3½fl oz) chicken stock
1 sheet leaf gelatine
freshly ground black pepper

1. Grease a 20.5cm (8in) springform cake tin with oil and put on a large baking tray. To make the pastry, put the flour and salt into a food processor. Next, melt the lard and 300ml (½ pint) water in a small pan and bring to the boil. With the motor of the processor running, add the hot lard mixture and whiz until the pastry nearly comes together. Tip on to a worksurface, bring together with your hands and knead until smooth.

2. Break off two-thirds of the pastry (put the remaining one-third to one side, uncovered) and roll out on a lightly floured surface until about 1cm (½ in) thick. Use to line the prepared tin, leaving some pastry hanging over the sides. Chill for 10 minutes. Cover the remaining pastry and put to one side at room temperature.

3. Preheat the oven to 180°C (160°C fan oven) mark 4. To make the filling, heat the oil in a small frying pan and gently cook the onion for 8 minutes until softened. Tip into a large bowl and leave to cool for a couple of minutes, then mix in the mince, bacon, mixed spice, parsley, ½ tsp salt and lots of ground black pepper.

4. Tip half the filling into the chilled pastry case and pat down firmly. Spread the onion marmalade over the filling and top with the remaining filling, pressing down as before.

5. Roll out the remaining pastry as before until large enough to cover the pie. Place on top of the filling, then trim and crimp the edges (ensure the crimped edge sits inside the perimeter of the tin or the pie will be hard to remove). Brush the top with some of the beaten egg (don't brush the outer edge of the crimping as the egg will make the pastry stick to the tin).

6. Bake for 40 minutes, then carefully unclip and remove the outside ring of the tin, leaving the pie on its base on the baking tray. Brush all over with egg and put back into the oven for 30–35 minutes to set the sides and cook through. Take out of the oven.

7. Pour the cold stock into a pan and add the gelatine leaf. Leave to soak for 5 minutes, then heat gently until the gelatine dissolves. Empty into a jug.

8. Filling the pie with the stock mixture isn't an essential step, but there'll be a gap between the meat and pastry if you don't. Use the tip of a knife or a skewer to poke a small hole in the top of the pie. Using a fine funnel (or a steady hand), pour a little stock into the hole and wait for it to be absorbed. Keep adding stock (and waiting for it to be absorbed) until the pie will take no more. Leave the pie to cool for 30 minutes, then chill overnight. Allow to come up to room temperature before serving.

Veal & Ham Pie

Preparation Time 45 minutes, plus chilling • Cooking Time about 3½ hours, plus cooling • Serves 12 •
Per Serving 617 calories, 37g fat (of which 14g saturates), 45g carbohydrate, 2g salt • A Little Effort

3 or 4 small veal bones
1 small onion
1 bay leaf
4 black peppercorns
700g (1½lb) diced pie veal
225g (8oz) diced cooked ham
1 tbsp freshly chopped flat-leafed
   parsley
grated zest and juice of 1 lemon
1 tbsp salt
½ tsp pepper
150ml (¼ pint) milk and 150ml
   (¼ pint) water mixed
150g (5oz) lard
450g (1lb) plain flour, plus extra
   to dust
1 medium egg, hard-boiled
1 medium egg, beaten
salad to serve

1. Put the bones, onion, bay leaf and peppercorns into a pan and cover with water. Simmer for 20 minutes, then boil to reduce the liquid to 150ml (¼ pint). Strain and cool. Base-line a 20.5cm (8in) springform cake tin.

2. Mix together the diced veal, diced ham, parsley, lemon zest and juice, 1 tsp salt and the pepper.

3. Bring the milk and water and the lard to the boil in a pan, then gradually beat it into the flour and remaining salt in a bowl. Knead for 3–4 minutes.

4. Roll out two-thirds of the pastry on a lightly floured surface and mould into the springform cake tin. Cover and chill for 30 minutes. Keep the remaining pastry covered. Preheat the oven to 220°C (200°C fan oven) mark 7.

5. Spoon half the meat mixture and 2 tbsp cold jellied stock into the pastry case. Put the hard-boiled egg in the centre and cover with the remaining meat mixture and 2 more tbsp cold jellied stock. Roll out the remaining pastry to make a lid and put on top of the meat mixture, sealing the pastry edges well. Decorate with pastry trimmings and make a hole in the centre. Glaze with the beaten egg.

6. Bake for 30 minutes. Cover loosely with foil, reduce the oven temperature to 180°C (160°C fan oven) mark 4 and bake for a further 2½ hours. Cool.

7. Warm the remaining jellied stock until liquid, then pour into the centre hole of the pie. Chill the pie, then unmould and serve with salad.

FREEZING TIP
To freeze Complete the recipe, then freeze the cooked pie whole, or in slices, wrapped in clingfilm for up to one month (wrapped slices can be stacked on top of each other).
To use Thaw in the fridge or at cool room temperature.

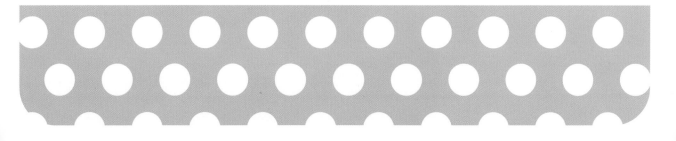

VEGETARIAN & VEGETABLES

Pumpkin Risotto with Hazelnut Butter

Preparation Time 15 minutes • Cooking Time 40 minutes • Serves 4 • Per Serving 706 calories, 50g fat (of which 27g saturates), 51g carbohydrate, 1.1g salt • Vegetarian • Gluten Free • Easy

50g (2oz) butter
175g (6oz) onion, finely chopped
900g (2lb) pumpkin, halved, peeled, seeded and cut into small cubes
2 garlic cloves, crushed
225g (8oz) risotto (arborio) rice
600ml (1 pint) hot stock
grated zest of ½ orange
40g (1½oz) freshly shaved vegetarian Parmesan (see Cook's Tips)
salt and ground black pepper

FOR THE HAZELNUT BUTTER
50g (2oz) hazelnuts
125g (4oz) softened butter
2 tbsp freshly chopped flat-leafed parsley

1. To make the hazelnut butter, spread the hazelnuts on a baking sheet and toast under a hot grill until golden brown, turning frequently. Put the nuts in a clean teatowel and rub off the skins, then chop finely. Put the nuts, butter and parsley on a piece of non-stick baking parchment. Season with pepper and mix together. Mould into a sausage shape, twist at both ends and chill.

2. To make the risotto, melt the butter in a large pan and fry the onion until soft but not coloured. Add the pumpkin and sauté over a low heat for 5–8 minutes until just beginning to soften. Add the garlic and rice and stir until well mixed. Increase the heat to medium and add the hot stock a little at a time, allowing the liquid to be absorbed after each addition. This will take about 25 minutes.

3. Stir in the orange zest and Parmesan and season with salt and pepper. Serve the risotto with a slice of the hazelnut butter melting on top.

COOK'S TIPS

• *If you can't find pumpkin, use butternut squash.*
• *Vegetarian cheeses: some vegetarians prefer to avoid cheeses that have been produced by the traditional method, because this uses animal-derived rennet. Most supermarkets and cheese shops now stock an excellent range of vegetarian cheeses, produced using vegetarian rennet, which comes from plants, such as thistle and mallow, that contain enzymes capable of curdling milk.*

Chickpea Curry

Preparation Time 20 minutes • Cooking Time 40–45 minutes • Serves 6 • Per Serving 291 calories,
8g fat (of which 1g saturates), 46g carbohydrate, 1.3g salt • Vegetarian • Gluten Free • Dairy Free • Easy

2 tbsp vegetable oil
2 onions, finely sliced
2 garlic cloves, crushed
1 tbsp ground coriander
1 tsp mild chilli powder
1 tbsp black mustard seeds
2 tbsp tamarind paste (see Cook's Tip)
2 tbsp sun-dried tomato paste
750g (1lb 11oz) new potatoes, quartered
400g can chopped tomatoes
1 litre (1¾ pints) hot vegetable stock
250g (9oz) green beans, trimmed
2 × 400g cans chickpeas, drained and rinsed
2 tsp garam masala
salt and ground black pepper

1. Heat the oil in a pan and fry the onions for 10–15 minutes until golden – when they have a good colour they will add depth of flavour. Add the garlic, coriander, chilli powder, mustard seeds, tamarind paste and sun-dried tomato paste. Cook for 1–2 minutes until the aroma from the spices is released.

2. Add the potatoes and toss in the spices for 1–2 minutes. Add the tomatoes and hot stock and season with salt and pepper. Cover and bring to the boil, then reduce the heat and simmer, half covered, for 20 minutes or until the potatoes are just cooked.

3. Add the beans and chickpeas and continue to cook for 5 minutes or until the beans are tender and the chickpeas are warmed through. Stir in the garam masala and serve.

COOK'S TIP
Tamarind paste has a very sharp, sour flavour and is widely used in Asian and South-east Asian cooking.

Aubergine & Lentil Curry

Preparation Time 10 minutes • Cooking Time 40–45 minutes • Serves 4 • Per Serving 335 calories, 15g fat (of which 3g saturates), 39g carbohydrate, 0.2g salt • Vegetarian • Easy

3 tbsp olive oil

2 aubergines, cut into 2.5cm (1in) chunks

1 onion, chopped

2 tbsp mild curry paste

3 × 400g cans chopped tomatoes

200ml (7fl oz) hot vegetable stock

150g (5oz) red lentils, rinsed

100g (3½oz) spinach leaves

25g (1oz) fresh coriander, roughly chopped

2 tbsp fat-free Greek yogurt

rice to serve (optional)

1. Heat 2 tbsp oil in a large pan over a low heat and fry the aubergine chunks until golden. Remove from the pan and put to one side.

2. Heat the remaining oil in the same pan and fry the onion for 8–10 minutes until soft. Add the curry paste and stir-fry for a further 2 minutes.

3. Add the tomatoes, hot stock, lentils and reserved aubergines to the pan. Bring to the boil, then reduce the heat to a low simmer, half-cover the pan with a lid and simmer for 25 minutes or according to the lentils' pack instructions.

4. At the end of cooking, stir the spinach, coriander and yogurt through the curry. Serve with rice, if you like.

COOK'S TIP

Choose aubergines that are firm, shiny and blemish-free, with a bright green stem.

Saag Aloo

Preparation Time 15 minutes • Cooking Time 55 minutes • Serves 4 • Per Serving 295 calories,
10g fat (of which 1g saturates), 47g carbohydrate, 0.2g salt • Vegetarian • Gluten Free • Dairy Free • Easy

2–3 tbsp vegetable oil
1 onion, finely sliced
2 garlic cloves, finely chopped
1 tbsp black mustard seeds
2 tsp ground turmeric
900g (2lb) potatoes, cut into 4cm
  (½in) chunks
1 tsp salt
4 handfuls of baby spinach leaves

1. Heat the oil in a pan and fry the onion over a medium heat for 10 minutes or until golden, taking care not to burn it.

2. Add the garlic, mustard seeds and turmeric and cook for 1 minute. Add the potatoes, salt and 150ml (¼ pint) water. Cover the pan and bring to the boil, then reduce the heat and cook gently for 35–40 minutes or until tender. Add the spinach and cook until the leaves just wilt. Serve immediately.

Lentil Casserole

Preparation Time 20 minutes • Cooking Time 1 hour • Serves 6 • Per Serving 239 calories,
6g fat (of which 1g saturates), 36g carbohydrate, 0.4g salt • Vegetarian • Gluten Free • Dairy Free • Easy

2 tbsp olive oil

2 onions, sliced

4 carrots, sliced

3 leeks, trimmed and sliced

450g (1lb) button mushrooms

2 garlic cloves, crushed

2.5cm (1in) piece fresh root ginger,
    peeled and grated

1 tbsp ground coriander

225g (8oz) split red lentils

750ml (1¼ pints) hot vegetable
    stock

4 tbsp freshly chopped coriander

salt and ground black pepper

1. Preheat the oven to 180°C
(160°C fan oven) mark 4. Heat the
oil in a flameproof ovenproof
casserole, add the onions, carrots
and leeks and fry, stirring, for
5 minutes. Add the mushrooms,
garlic, ginger and ground coriander
and fry for 2–3 minutes.

2. Rinse and drain the lentils, then
stir into the casserole with the hot
stock. Season with salt and pepper
and return to the boil. Cover and
cook in the oven for 45–50 minutes
until the vegetables and lentils are
tender. Stir in the chopped
coriander before serving.

Moroccan Chickpea Stew

Preparation Time 10 minutes • Cooking Time 40 minutes • Serves 4 • Per Serving 232 calories,
9g fat (of which 1g saturates), 29g carbohydrate, 0.6g salt • Vegetarian • Dairy Free • Easy

1 red pepper, halved and seeded
1 green pepper, halved and seeded
1 yellow pepper, halved and seeded
2 tbsp olive oil
1 onion, finely sliced
2 garlic cloves, crushed
1 tbsp harissa paste
2 tbsp tomato purée
½ tsp ground cumin
1 aubergine, diced
400g can chickpeas, drained and
   rinsed
450ml (¾ pint) vegetable stock
4 tbsp roughly chopped fresh flat-
   leafed parsley, plus a few sprigs
   to garnish
salt and ground black pepper

1. Preheat the grill and lay the
peppers, skin side up, on a baking
sheet. Grill for around 5 minutes
until the skin begins to blister and
char. Put the peppers into a plastic
bag, seal and put to one side for
a few minutes. When cooled a little,
peel off the skins and discard,
then slice the peppers and put
to one side.

2. Heat the oil in a large heavy-
based frying pan over a low heat,
add the onion and cook for
5–10 minutes until soft. Add the
garlic, harissa, tomato purée and
cumin and cook for 2 minutes.

3. Add the peppers to the pan
with the aubergine. Stir everything
to coat evenly with the spices
and cook for 2 minutes. Add the
chickpeas and stock, season well
with salt and pepper and bring to
the boil. Reduce the heat and
simmer for 20 minutes.

4. Just before serving, stir the
parsley through the chickpea stew.
Serve in warmed bowls, garnished
with parsley sprigs.

Baked Tomatoes & Fennel

Preparation Time 10 minutes • Cooking Time 1¼ hours • Serves 6 • Per Serving 127 calories,
9g fat (of which 1g saturates), 7g carbohydrate, 0.1g salt • Vegetarian • Gluten Free • Dairy Free • Easy

**900g (2lb) fennel, trimmed and cut
  into quarters**
75ml (2½fl oz) white wine
5 thyme sprigs
75ml (2½fl oz) olive oil
**900g (2lb) ripe beef or plum
  tomatoes**

1. Preheat the oven to 200°C
(180°C fan oven) mark 6. Put the
fennel into a roasting tin and pour
the wine over it. Snip the thyme
sprigs over the fennel, drizzle with
the oil and roast for 45 minutes.

2. Halve the tomatoes, add to
the roasting tin and continue
to roast for 30 minutes or until
tender, basting with the juices
halfway through.

COOK'S TIP
*This is an ideal accompaniment to
grilled fish or meat, or a vegetarian
frittata.*

Roasted Ratatouille

Preparation Time 15 minutes • Cooking Time 1½ hours • Serves 6 • Per Serving 224 calories,
18g fat (of which 3g saturates), 14g carbohydrate, 0g salt • Vegetarian • Gluten Free • Dairy Free • Easy

**400g (14oz) red peppers, seeded
and roughly chopped**
**700g (1½lb) aubergines, cut into
chunks**
450g (1lb) onions, cut into wedges
**4 or 5 garlic cloves, unpeeled and
left whole**
150ml (¼ pint) olive oil
1 tsp fennel seeds
200ml (7fl oz) passata
**sea salt flakes and ground black
pepper**
a few fresh thyme sprigs to garnish

1. Preheat the oven to 240°C (220°C fan oven) mark 9. Put the peppers, aubergines, onions, garlic, oil and fennel seeds into a roasting tin. Season with sea salt flakes and pepper and toss together.

2. Transfer to the oven and cook for 30 minutes (tossing frequently during cooking) or until the vegetables are charred and beginning to soften.

3. Stir the passata through the vegetables and put the roasting tin back in the oven for 50–60 minutes, stirring occasionally. Garnish with the thyme sprigs and serve.

TRY SOMETHING DIFFERENT
Replace half the aubergines with 400g (14oz) courgettes; use a mix of green and red peppers; garnish with fresh basil instead of thyme.

Leek & Broccoli Bake

Preparation Time 20 minutes • Cooking Time 45–55 minutes • Serves 4 • Per Serving 245 calories, 13g fat (of which 4g saturates), 18g carbohydrate, 0.4g salt • Vegetarian • Gluten Free • Easy

2 tbsp olive oil

1 large red onion, cut into wedges

1 aubergine, chopped

2 leeks, trimmed and cut into chunks

1 broccoli head, cut into florets and stalks chopped

3 large flat mushrooms, chopped

2 × 400g cans cherry tomatoes

3 rosemary sprigs, chopped

50g (2oz) vegetarian Parmesan, freshly grated (optional, see page 140)

salt and ground black pepper

1. Preheat the oven to 200°C (180°C fan oven) mark 6. Heat the oil in a large flameproof dish, add the onion, aubergine and leeks and cook for 10–12 minutes until golden and softened.

2. Add the broccoli, mushrooms, cherry tomatoes, half the rosemary and 300ml (½ pint) boiling water. Season with salt and pepper. Stir well, then cover and cook in the oven for 30 minutes.

3. Meanwhile, put the Parmesan into a bowl, if using. Add the remaining rosemary and season with pepper. When the vegetables are cooked, remove the lid and sprinkle the Parmesan mixture on top. Cook, uncovered, in the oven for a further 5–10 minutes until the topping is golden.

TRY SOMETHING DIFFERENT

Use sliced courgettes instead of aubergine.

Caramelised Onion & Goat's Cheese Tart

Preparation Time 10 minutes • Cooking Time 1 hour • Serves 6 • Per Serving 480 calories, 28g fat (of which 14g saturates), 44g carbohydrate, 1.5g salt • Vegetarian • Easy

230g ready-made shortcrust pastry case
275g jar onion confit
300g (11oz) mild soft goat's cheese
1 medium egg, beaten
25g (1oz) freshly grated vegetarian Parmesan (see page 140)
50g (2oz) wild rocket
balsamic vinegar and extra virgin olive oil to drizzle
salt and ground black pepper

1. Preheat the oven to 200°C (180°C fan oven) mark 6. Line the pastry case with greaseproof paper, fill with baking beans and bake blind (see Cook's Tip) for 10 minutes. Remove the paper and beans, prick the pastry base all over with a fork and cook for a further 15–20 minutes until golden.

2. Spoon the onion confit into the pastry case. Beat the goat's cheese and egg together in a bowl until smooth, season with salt and pepper, then spoon on top of the onions. Level the surface with a knife and sprinkle the Parmesan over. Cook the tart for 25–30 minutes until the filling is set and just beginning to turn golden.

3. Leave to cool for 15 minutes, then cut away the sides of the foil case and carefully slide the tart on to a plate. Just before serving, arrange the rocket on top of the tart and drizzle with balsamic vinegar and olive oil. Serve warm.

COOK'S TIP
Baking blind
Cooking the pastry before filling gives a crisp result. Preheat the oven according to the recipe. Prick the pastry base with a fork. Cover with foil or greaseproof paper 7.5cm (3in) larger than the tin. Spread baking beans on top. Bake for 15–20 minutes. Remove the foil or paper and beans and bake for 5–10 minutes until the pastry is light golden. When cooked and while still hot, brush the base of the pastry with a little beaten egg, to seal the fork pricks or any cracks. This will prevent any filling leaking, which can make it difficult to remove the pie or tart from the tin.

Roasted Vegetable Salad with Mustard Mayonnaise

Preparation Time 15 minutes • Cooking Time 40 minutes • Serves 4 • Per Serving 420 calories, 43g fat (of which 6g saturates), 5g carbohydrate, 1g salt • Vegetarian • Gluten Free • Dairy Free • Easy

900g (2lb) mixed vegetables, such as fennel, courgettes, leeks, aubergines, baby turnips, new potatoes and red onions
2 garlic cloves, unpeeled
4–5 fresh marjoram or rosemary sprigs
5 tbsp olive oil
1 tsp sea salt flakes
mixed crushed peppercorns to taste
4 tsp balsamic vinegar
warm crusty bread to serve

FOR THE MUSTARD MAYONNAISE
150ml (¼ pint) mayonnaise
2 tbsp Dijon mustard
salt and ground black pepper

1. Preheat the oven to 220°C (200°C fan oven) mark 7. For the vegetables, quarter the fennel, chop the courgettes, leeks and aubergines, trim the turnips and cut the onions into petals. Place the vegetables, garlic, marjoram or rosemary, the oil, salt and peppercorns in a roasting tin and toss well (see Cook's Tip).

2. Cook in the oven for 30–35 minutes or until the vegetables are golden, tossing frequently. Sprinkle the vinegar over and return to the oven for a further 5 minutes.

3. To make the mustard mayonnaise, mix the mayonnaise with the mustard, then season with salt and pepper and set aside.

4. Arrange the vegetable salad on a serving dish and serve with the mustard mayonnaise and crusty bread.

COOK'S TIP
It's best to roast vegetables in a single layer or they will steam and become soggy. Use two tins if necessary

Aubergines in a Hot Sweet & Sour Sauce

Preparation Time 10 minutes • Cooking Time 35 minutes • Serves 4 • Per Serving 136 calories, 7g fat (of which 1g saturates), 17g carbohydrate, 2.5g salt • Vegetarian • Gluten Free • Dairy Free • Easy

3 tbsp vegetable oil

200g (7oz) onions, thinly sliced

2.5cm (1in) piece fresh root ginger, peeled and finely chopped

2 red chillies, finely chopped (see page 30), plus extra whole red chillies to garnish (optional)

1½ tsp cumin seeds

1¼ tsp coriander seeds

3 cloves

5cm (2in) cinnamon stick

1 tbsp paprika

juice of 2 limes

3–4 tbsp dark muscovado sugar

1–2 tsp salt

450g (1lb) aubergines, cut into 2.5cm (1in) pieces

rice to serve

1. Heat the oil in a wok or large frying pan, add the onions, ginger and chopped chillies and stir-fry for about 4 minutes or until softened. Add the cumin and coriander seeds, cloves and cinnamon and cook for 2–3 minutes.

2. Add 300ml (½ pint) water to the pan, then stir in the paprika, lime juice, sugar, salt and aubergines. Bring to the boil, then reduce the heat and simmer, covered, for about 20 minutes or until the aubergines are tender.

3. Uncover the pan and bring the sauce back to the boil. Bubble for 3–4 minutes until the liquid is thick enough to coat the aubergine pieces. Serve with rice, garnished with whole red chillies, if you like.

TRY SOMETHING DIFFERENT

Braised Aubergines

Omit the cumin, coriander, cloves, cinnamon and paprika. Add the aubergines to the onion mixture at the end of step 1 and stir-fry for 1–2 minutes. Add 1 tbsp sugar, 1 tsp salt, 3–4 tbsp yellow bean sauce and the water, then complete the recipe.

FOR THE
SLOW COOKER

Carrot & Coriander Soup

Preparation Time 15 minutes • Cooking Time 15 minutes in pan, then about 4 hours on High, plus cooling • Serves 6 • Per Serving 140 calories, 11g fat (of which 7g saturates), 10g carbohydrate, 0.2g salt • Easy

40g (1½oz) butter

175g (6oz) leeks, trimmed and sliced

450g (1lb) carrots, sliced

2 tsp ground coriander

1 tsp plain flour

1 litre (1¾ pints) hot vegetable stock

150ml (¼ pint) single cream

salt and freshly ground black pepper

fresh coriander leaves, roughly torn, to serve

1. Melt the butter in a large pan. Stir in the leeks and carrots, then cover the pan and cook gently for 7–10 minutes until the vegetables begin to soften but not colour.

2. Stir in the ground coriander and flour and cook, stirring, for 1 minute.

3. Add the hot stock and bring to the boil, stirring. Season with salt and ground black pepper, then transfer to the slow cooker, cover and cook on High for 3–4 hours until the vegetables are tender.

4. Leave the soup to cool a little, then whiz in batches in a blender or food processor until smooth. Pour into a clean pan and stir in the cream. Adjust the seasoning and reheat gently on the hob – do not boil. Ladle into warmed bowls, scatter with torn coriander leaves and serve.

Beetroot Soup

Preparation Time 15 minutes • Cooking Time 15 minutes in pan, then about 4 hours on High • Serves 8 •
Per Serving 290 calories, 25g fat (of which 4g saturates), 15g carbohydrate, 0.2g salt • Easy

1 tbsp olive oil

1 onion, finely chopped

750g (1lb 11oz) raw beetroot, peeled and cut into 1cm (½in) cubes

275g (10oz) potatoes, roughly chopped

1.5 litres (2½ pints) hot vegetable stock

juice of 1 lemon

salt and freshly ground black pepper

TO SERVE

125ml (4fl oz) soured cream

25g (1oz) mixed root vegetable crisps (optional)

2 tbsp snipped fresh chives

1. Heat the oil in a large pan. Add the onion and cook for 5 minutes to soften. Add the beetroot and potatoes and cook for a further 5 minutes.

2. Add the hot stock and the lemon juice and bring to the boil. Season with salt and ground black pepper, then transfer to the slow cooker, cover and cook on High for 3–4 hours until the beetroot is tender.

3. Leave the soup to cool a little, then whiz in batches in a blender or food processor until smooth. Pour into a clean pan and reheat gently on the hob – do not boil. Ladle into warmed bowls. Swirl 1 tbsp soured cream on each portion, scatter with a few vegetable crisps, if you like, and sprinkle with snipped chives to serve.

FREEZING TIP

To freeze Complete the recipe to the end of step 2, then cool half or all the soup, pack and freeze for up to three months.

To use Thaw the soup overnight and simmer over a low heat for 5 minutes.

French Onion Soup

Preparation Time 30 minutes • Cooking Time 40 minutes in pan, then about 4 hours on Low • Serves 4 •
Per Serving 438 calories, 21g fat (of which 13g saturates), 45g carbohydrate, 1.3g salt • Easy

75g (3oz) butter
700g (1½lb) onions, sliced
3 garlic cloves, crushed
1 tbsp plain flour
200ml (7fl oz) dry white wine
1 litre (1¾ pints) hot vegetable
   stock
bouquet garni (1 bay leaf, a few
   fresh thyme and parsley sprigs)
salt and freshly ground black
   pepper

TO SERVE
1 small baguette, cut into slices
   1cm (½in) thick
50g (2oz) Gruyère cheese or
   Cheddar, grated

1. Melt the butter in a large pan.
Add the onions and cook slowly
over a very low heat, stirring
frequently, until very soft and
golden brown – this should take
at least 30 minutes. Add the garlic
and flour and cook, stirring, for
1 minute.

2. Pour in the wine and let bubble
until reduced by half. Add the hot
stock, the bouquet garni and
seasoning and bring to the boil.
Transfer to the slow cooker, cover
and cook on Low for 3–4 hours until
the onions are meltingly tender.

3. When ready to serve, preheat
the grill. Lightly toast the slices of
baguette on both sides. Reheat
the soup and adjust the seasoning.
Discard the bouquet garni.

4. Divide the soup among four
ovenproof soup bowls. Float two or
three slices of toast on each portion
and sprinkle thickly with the grated
cheese. Stand the bowls under
the hot grill until the cheese has
melted and turned golden brown.
Serve at once.

Leek & Potato Soup

Preparation Time 10 minutes • Cooking Time 30 minutes in pan, then about 4 hours on Low, plus cooling • Serves 4 • Per Serving 117 calories, 6g fat (of which 4g saturates), 13g carbohydrate, 0.1g salt • Easy

25g (1oz) butter
1 onion, finely chopped
1 garlic clove, crushed
550g (1¼lb) leeks, trimmed and chopped
200g (7oz) floury potatoes, sliced
1.1 litres (2 pints) hot vegetable stock
crème fraîche and chopped chives to garnish

1. Melt the butter in a pan over a gentle heat. Add the onion and cook for 10–15 minutes until soft. Add the garlic and cook for a further 1 minute. Add the leeks and cook for 5–10 minutes until softened. Add the potatoes and toss together with the leeks.

2. Pour in the hot stock and bring to the boil. Transfer the soup to the slow cooker, cover and cook on Low for 3–4 hours until the potatoes are tender.

3. Leave the soup to cool a little, then whiz in batches in a blender or food processor until smooth.

4. Pour the soup into a clean pan and reheat gently on the hob – do not boil. Ladle into warmed bowls, garnish with crème fraîche and chives and serve.

Mexican Bean Soup

Preparation Time 15 minutes • Cooking Time 2–3 hours on High • Serves 6 • Per Serving without lime butter
184 calories, 8g fat (of which 1g saturates), 21g carbohydrate, 1.3g salt • Vegetarian • Dairy Free • Easy

4 tbsp olive oil
1 onion, chopped
2 garlic cloves, chopped
a pinch of crushed red chillies
1 tsp ground coriander
1 tsp ground cumin
1/2 tsp ground cinnamon
600ml (1 pint) hot vegetable stock
300ml (1/2 pint) tomato juice
1–2 tsp chilli sauce

2 × 400g cans red kidney beans,
**   drained and rinsed**
2 tbsp freshly chopped coriander
salt and ground black pepper
coriander leaves, roughly torn,
**   to garnish**
lime butter to serve (optional, see
**   Cook's Tip)**

1. Heat the oil in a large pan, add the onion, garlic, chillies and spices and fry gently for 5 minutes or until lightly golden.

2. Add the hot stock, the tomato juice, chilli sauce and beans and bring to the boil, then transfer to the slow cooker, cover and cook on High for 2–3 hours.

3. Leave the soup to cool a little, then whiz in batches in a blender or food processor until very smooth. Pour the soup into a pan, stir in the chopped coriander and heat through, then season to taste with salt and pepper.

4. Ladle the soup into warmed bowls. Top each portion with a few slices of lime butter, if you like, and scatter with torn coriander leaves.

COOK'S TIP
Lime Butter
Beat the grated zest and juice of 1/2 lime into 50g (2oz) softened butter and season to taste with salt and pepper. Shape into a log, wrap in clingfilm and chill until needed. To serve, unwrap and slice thinly.

Scotch Broth

Preparation Time 15 minutes • Cooking Time 8–10 hours on Low • Serves 8 • Per Serving 173 calories, 2g fat (of which trace saturates), 35g carbohydrate, 2.3g salt • Dairy Free • Easy

1.4kg (3lb) piece beef skirt (ask your butcher for this)
300g (11oz) broth mix (to include pearl barley, red lentils, split peas and green peas), soaked according to the pack instructions
2 carrots, finely chopped
1 parsnip, finely chopped
2 onions, finely chopped

¼ white cabbage, finely chopped
1 leek, trimmed and finely chopped
1 piece marrow bone, about 350g (12oz)
½ tbsp salt
ground black pepper
2 tbsp freshly chopped parsley to serve

1. Put the beef into a large pan and cover with water. Slowly bring to the boil, then reduce the heat and simmer for 10 minutes, using a slotted spoon to remove any scum that comes to the surface. Drain.

2. Put the broth mix and all the vegetables into the slow cooker, then place the beef and marrow bone on top. Add 1.5 litres (2½ pints) boiling water – there should be enough to just cover the meat. Cover and cook on Low for 8–10 hours until the meat is tender.

3. Remove the marrow bone and beef from the broth. Add a few shreds of beef to the broth, if you like. Season the broth well with the salt and some pepper, stir in the chopped parsley and serve hot.

COOK'S TIP

This can be two meals in one: a starter and a main course. The beef flavours the stock and is removed before serving. You can then divide up the meat and serve it with mashed potatoes, swedes or turnips.

Split Pea & Ham Soup

Preparation Time 15 minutes, plus overnight soaking • Cooking Time 20 minutes in pan, then about 4 hours on High, plus cooling • Serves 6 • Per Serving 400 calories, 10g fat (of which 5g saturates), 53g carbohydrate, 1.5g salt • Easy

500g pack of dried yellow split peas, soaked overnight (see Cook's Tip)
25g (1oz) butter
1 large onion, finely chopped
125g (4oz) rindless smoked streaky bacon rashers, roughly chopped
1 garlic clove, crushed
1.7 litres (3 pints) well-flavoured ham or vegetable stock
1 bouquet garni (1 bay leaf, a few fresh parsley and thyme sprigs)
1 tsp dried oregano
125g (4oz) chopped cooked ham
salt and freshly ground black pepper
cracked black pepper to serve

1. Drain the soaked split peas. Melt the butter in a large pan, add the onion, bacon and garlic and cook over a low heat for about 10 minutes until the onion is soft.

2. Add the split peas to the pan with the stock. Bring to the boil and use a slotted spoon to remove any scum that comes to the surface. Add the bouquet garni and oregano, then season with salt and ground black pepper. Transfer to the slow cooker, cover and cook on High for 3–4 hours until the peas are very soft.

3. Leave the soup to cool a little, then whiz half the soup in a blender or food processor until smooth. Pour all the soup into a clean pan and reheat gently on the hob – do not boil. Add the ham and check the seasoning. Ladle into warmed bowls and sprinkle with cracked black pepper to serve.

COOK'S TIP

Dried peas form the base of this comforting soup and are much cheaper than canned peas. First, you need to soak them overnight in about 1 litre (1¾ pints) cold water. If you forget, put them straight into a pan with the water, bring to the boil and cook for 1–2 minutes, then leave to stand for 2 hours before using.

Braised Chicory in White Wine

Preparation Time 5 minutes • Cooking Time about 3 hours on Low • Serves 4 •
Per Serving 80 calories, 7g fat (of which 5g saturates), 3g carbohydrate, 0.1g salt • Easy

50g (2oz) butter, softened
6 chicory heads, trimmed
juice of ½ lemon
100ml (3½fl oz) white wine
salt and freshly ground black
**   pepper**
snipped fresh chives to serve

1. Grease the slow cooker dish with 15g (½oz) of the butter. Toss the chicory in the lemon juice and arrange in the bottom of the dish.

2. Season to taste, add the wine and dot the remaining butter over the top. Cover and cook on Low for 2–3 hours until soft. Scatter with chives to serve.

Spiced Bean & Vegetable Stew

Preparation Time 15 minutes • Cooking Time 2–3 hours on Low • Serves 6 • Per Serving 262 calories,
7g fat (of which 1g saturates), 44g carbohydrate, 1.3g salt • Vegetarian • Gluten Free • Dairy Free • Easy

3 tbsp olive oil
2 small onions, sliced
2 garlic cloves, crushed
1 tbsp sweet paprika
1 small dried red chilli, seeded and
 finely chopped
700g (1½lb) sweet potatoes, cubed
700g (1½lb) pumpkin, cut into
 chunks
125g (4oz) okra, trimmed
500g jar passata
400g can haricot or cannellini
 beans, drained and rinsed
450ml (¾ pint) hot vegetable stock
salt and ground black pepper

1. Heat the oil in a large pan over
a very gentle heat. Add the onions
and garlic and cook for 5 minutes.

2. Stir in the paprika and chilli
and cook for 2 minutes, then add
the sweet potatoes, pumpkin, okra,
passata, beans and hot stock.
Season generously with salt and
pepper and bring to the boil.

3. Transfer to the slow cooker, cover
and cook on Low for 2–3 hours until
the vegetables are tender.

**TRY SOMETHING
DIFFERENT**
*Instead of paprika, use 1 tsp each
ground cumin and ground
coriander. Garnish with freshly
chopped coriander.*

Mushroom & Bean Hotpot

Preparation Time 15 minutes • Cooking Time 2–3 hours on Low • Serves 6 • Per Serving 280 calories, 10g fat (of which 1g saturates), 34g carbohydrate, 1.3g salt • Vegetarian • Dairy Free • Easy

3 tbsp olive oil

700g (1½lb) chestnut mushrooms, roughly chopped

1 large onion, finely chopped

2 tbsp plain flour

2 tbsp mild curry paste

150ml (¼ pint) dry white wine

400g can chopped tomatoes

2 tbsp sun-dried tomato paste

2 × 400g cans mixed beans, drained and rinsed

3 tbsp mango chutney

3 tbsp roughly chopped fresh coriander and mint

1. Heat the oil in a large pan over a low heat and fry the mushrooms and onion until the onion is soft and dark golden. Then stir in the flour and curry paste and cook for 1–2 minutes. Add the wine, tomatoes, sun-dried tomato paste and beans.

2. Bring to the boil, then transfer to the slow cooker. Cover and cook on Low for 2–3 hours.

3. Stir in the chutney and herbs and serve.

Lentils with Red Pepper

Preparation Time 10 minutes • Cooking Time 3–4 hours on High • Serves 4 • Per Serving 296 calories, 5g fat (of which 1g saturates), 47g carbohydrate, 0.1g salt • Vegetarian • Gluten Free • Dairy Free • Easy

1 tbsp olive oil

1 large onion, finely chopped

2 celery sticks, diced

2 carrots, diced

2 bay leaves, torn

300g (11oz) Puy lentils

600ml (1 pint) hot vegetable stock

1 marinated red pepper, drained
   and chopped

2 tbsp chopped flat-leafed parsley,
   plus extra to garnish

ground black pepper

1. Heat the oil in a pan, add the onion and cook over a low heat for 15 minutes or until soft. Add the celery, carrots and bay leaves and cook for 2 minutes.

2. Add the lentils with the hot stock and stir everything together. Transfer to the slow cooker, cover and cook on High for 3–4 hours.

3. Stir in the red pepper and parsley and season with pepper. Leave to stand for 10 minutes, then garnish with extra parsley and serve as an accompaniment.

Ratatouille

Preparation Time 20 minutes • Cooking Time 3–4 hours on High • Serves 6 • Per Serving 150 calories,
9g fat (of which 1g saturates), 15g carbohydrate, 0.1g salt • Vegetarian • Gluten Free • Dairy Free • Easy

4 tbsp olive oil

2 onions, thinly sliced

1 large garlic clove, crushed

350g (12oz) small aubergines, thinly sliced

450g (1lb) small courgettes, thinly sliced

450g (1lb) tomatoes, skinned, seeded and roughly chopped

1 green and 1 red pepper, each cored, seeded and sliced

1 tbsp chopped basil

2 tsp freshly chopped thyme

2 tbsp freshly chopped flat-leafed parsley

2 tbsp sun-dried tomato paste

salt and ground black pepper

1. Heat the oil in a large pan, add the onions and garlic and fry gently for 10 minutes or until softened and golden.

2. Add the aubergines, courgettes, tomatoes, sliced peppers, herbs, tomato paste and seasoning. Fry, stirring, for 2–3 minutes.

3. Transfer to the slow cooker and cover. Cook on High for 3–4 hours until all the vegetables are tender. Taste and adjust the seasoning. Serve the ratatouille hot or at room temperature.

Braised Red Cabbage

Preparation Time 10 minutes • Cooking Time 2–3 hours on Low • Serves 8 • Per Serving 50 calories, trace fat, 11g carbohydrate, 0g salt • Vegetarian • Gluten Free • Dairy Free • Easy

½ medium red cabbage, about
   500g (1lb 2oz), shredded
1 red onion, finely chopped
1 Bramley apple, peeled, cored and
   chopped
25g (1oz) light muscovado sugar
1 cinnamon stick

a pinch of ground cloves
¼ tsp freshly grated nutmeg
2 tbsp each red wine vinegar and
   red wine
juice of 1 orange
salt and ground black pepper

1. Put all the ingredients into the slow cooker and stir to mix well. Cover and cook on Low for 2–3 hours.

2. When the cabbage is tender, remove the pan from the heat and discard the cinnamon stick. Serve at once, or cool, put into a bowl, cover and chill the cabbage overnight.

3. To reheat, put the cabbage into a pan, add 2 tbsp cold water and cover with a tight-fitting lid. Bring to the boil, then reduce the heat and simmer for 25 minutes.

Easy Chicken Casserole

Preparation Time 15 minutes • Cooking Time 5–6 hours on Low • Serves 6 • Per Serving 323 calories,
18g fat (of which 5g saturates), 17g carbohydrate, 0.9g salt • Gluten Free • Dairy Free • Easy

1 tbsp sunflower oil

1 small chicken, about 1.4kg (3lb)

1 fresh rosemary sprig

2 bay leaves

1 red onion, cut into wedges

2 carrots, cut into chunks

2 leeks, trimmed and cut into chunks

2 celery sticks, cut into chunks

12 baby new potatoes, halved if large

900ml (1½ pints) hot chicken stock

200g (7oz) green beans, trimmed

salt and ground black pepper

1. Heat the oil in a large pan over a medium heat. Add the chicken and fry until browned all over. Put the chicken into the slow cooker, along with the herbs and all the vegetables except the green beans. Season well.

2. Pour in the hot stock, cover and cook on Low for 5–6 hours until the chicken is cooked through. Add the beans for the last hour or cook separately in lightly salted boiling water and stir into the casserole once it's cooked. To test the chicken is cooked, pierce the thickest part of the leg with a knife: the juices should run clear.

3. Remove the chicken and spoon the vegetables into six bowls. Carve the chicken and divide among the bowls, then ladle the cooking liquid over.

TRY SOMETHING DIFFERENT
Omit the baby new potatoes and serve with mashed potatoes.

Spanish Chicken

Preparation Time 25 minutes, plus infusing • Cooking Time 1–2 hours on Low • Serves 4 • Per Serving 671 calories, 28g fat (of which 5g saturates), 70g carbohydrate, 0.8g salt • Gluten Free • Dairy Free • Easy

1 tsp ground turmeric
1.1 litres (2 pints) hot chicken stock
2 tbsp vegetable oil
4 boneless, skinless chicken
   thighs, roughly diced
1 onion, chopped
1 red pepper, seeded and sliced
50g (2oz) chorizo sausage, diced
2 garlic cloves, crushed
300g (11oz) long-grain rice
125g (4oz) frozen peas
salt and ground black pepper
3 tbsp chopped flat-leafed parsley
   to garnish
crusty bread to serve

1. Add the turmeric to the hot stock and leave to infuse for at least 5 minutes. Meanwhile, heat the oil in a large frying pan over a medium heat. Add the chicken and fry for 10 minutes or until golden, then transfer to the slow cooker.

2. Add the onion to the pan and cook over a medium heat for 5 minutes or until soft. Add the red pepper and chorizo and cook for a further 5 minutes, then add the garlic and cook for 1 minute.

3. Add the rice and mix well. Pour in the stock and peas and season, then transfer to the slow cooker and stir together. Cover and cook on Low for 1–2 hours until the rice is tender and the chicken is cooked through.

4. Check the seasoning and garnish with the parsley. Serve with some crusty bread.

Chicken Tagine with Apricots & Almonds

Preparation Time 10 minutes • Cooking Time 4–5 hours on Low • Serves 4 • Per Serving 376 calories, 22g fat (of which 4g saturates), 19g carbohydrate, 0.5g salt • Gluten Free • Dairy Free • Easy

2 tbsp olive oil
4 chicken thighs
1 onion, chopped
2 tsp ground cinnamon
2 tbsp runny honey
150g (5oz) dried apricots
75g (3oz) blanched almonds
125ml (4fl oz) hot chicken stock
salt and ground black pepper
flaked almonds to garnish
couscous to serve

1. Heat 1 tbsp oil in a large pan over a medium heat. Add the chicken and fry for 5 minutes or until brown, then transfer to the slow cooker.

2. Add the onion to the pan with the remaining oil and fry for 10 minutes or until softened.

3. Add the cinnamon, honey, apricots, almonds and hot stock to the onion and season well. Bring to the boil, then transfer to the slow cooker, cover and cook on Low for 4–5 hours until the chicken is tender and cooked through. Garnish with the flaked almonds and serve hot with couscous.

Chicken with Chorizo & Beans

Preparation Time 10 minutes • Cooking Time 4–5 hours on Low • Serves 6 • Per Serving 690 calories, 41g fat (of which 12g saturates), 33g carbohydrate, 2.6g salt • Dairy Free • Easy

1 tbsp olive oil
12 chicken pieces (6 drumsticks
 and 6 thighs)
175g (6oz) chorizo sausage, cubed
1 onion, finely chopped
2 large garlic cloves, crushed
1 tsp mild chilli powder
3 red peppers, seeded and roughly
 chopped
400g (14oz) passata
2 tbsp tomato purée
150ml (¼ pint) hot chicken stock
2 × 400g cans butter beans, drained
 and rinsed
200g (7oz) new potatoes, quartered
1 small bunch of thyme
1 bay leaf
200g (7oz) baby leaf spinach

1. Heat the oil in a large pan over a medium heat. Add the chicken and fry until browned all over, then transfer to the slow cooker.

2. Add the chorizo to the pan and fry for 2–3 minutes until its oil starts to run. Add the onion, garlic and chilli powder and fry over a low heat for 5 minutes or until the onion is soft.

3. Add the red peppers and cook for 2–3 minutes until soft. Stir in the passata, tomato purée, hot stock, butter beans, potatoes, thyme sprigs and bay leaf. Bring to the boil, then add to the chicken. Cover and cook on Low for 4–5 hours until the chicken is cooked through.

4. Remove the thyme and bay leaf, then stir in the spinach until it wilts. Serve immediately.

TRY SOMETHING DIFFERENT
Use mixed beans instead of the butter beans.

Fruity Guinea Fowl

Preparation Time 40 minutes, plus marinating • Cooking Time about 25 minutes in pan, then about 6 hours on Low •
Serves 6 • Per Serving 620 calories, 21g fat (of which 6g saturates), 24g carbohydrate, 1.7g salt • Easy

225g (8oz) onion, roughly chopped
125g (4oz) carrot, chopped
125g (4oz) celery, chopped
6–8 guinea fowl joints, total weight
    2kg (4½lb)
750ml (1¼ pints) red wine
1 tsp black peppercorns, crushed
1 tbsp freshly chopped thyme
2 bay leaves
175g (6oz) ready-to-eat dried
    prunes
3 tbsp vegetable oil
225g (8oz) streaky bacon rashers,
    cut into strips
3 garlic cloves, crushed
1 tsp harissa paste
1 tbsp tomato purée
2 tbsp plain flour
300ml (½ pint) chicken stock
2 apples
salt and freshly ground black
    pepper
mashed potatoes to serve

1. Put the onion, carrot, celery, guinea fowl, 600ml (1 pint) of the wine, the peppercorns, thyme and bay leaves into a large bowl. Cover, chill and leave to marinate for at least 3–4 hours. Soak the prunes in the remaining wine for 3–4 hours.

2. Preheat the oven to 170°C (150°C fan oven) mark 3. Drain and dry the joints (put the vegetables and wine to one side). Heat 2 tbsp of the oil in a large pan. Brown the joints in batches, over a medium heat, then transfer to the slow cooker.

3. Add the marinated vegetables and the bacon to the pan (keep the marinade to one side) and stir-fry for 5 minutes. Add the garlic, harissa and tomato purée and cook for 1 minute. Mix in the flour and cook for 1 minute. Pour in the reserved marinade and stock and bring to the boil, stirring, then pour into the slow cooker and season well. Cover and cook on Low for 4–6 hours until the guinea fowl is cooked through.

4. Heat the remaining oil in a pan. Core and slice the apples, then cook for 2–3 minutes on each side until golden. Put to one side.

5. Remove the joints from the slow cooker. Strain the sauce and put back into the slow cooker with the joints. Add the prunes and any juices and the apple. Leave to stand for 10 minutes. Serve with mashed potatoes.

Mexican Chilli Con Carne

Preparation Time 5 minutes • Cooking Time 4–5 hours on Low • Serves 4 • Per Serving 408 calories, 19g fat (of which 7g saturates), 28g carbohydrate, 1.1g salt • Gluten Free • Dairy Free • Easy

2 tbsp olive oil

450g (1lb) minced beef

1 large onion, finely chopped

½–1 tsp each hot chilli powder and ground cumin

3 tbsp tomato purée

150ml (¼ pint) hot beef stock

400g can chopped tomatoes with garlic (see Cook's Tips)

25g (1oz) dark chocolate

400g can red kidney beans, drained and rinsed

2 × 20g packs coriander, chopped

salt and ground black pepper

guacamole, salsa (see page 90), soured cream, grated cheese, tortilla chips and pickled chillies to serve

1. Heat 1 tbsp oil in a large pan and fry the beef for 10 minutes or until well browned, stirring to break up any lumps. Remove from the pan with a slotted spoon and transfer to the slow cooker.

2. Add the remaining oil to the pan, then fry the onion, stirring, for 10 minutes or until soft and golden.

3. Add the spices and fry for 1 minute, then add the tomato purée, hot stock and the tomatoes. Bring to the boil, then stir into the mince in the slow cooker. Cover and cook on Low for 4–5 hours.

4. Stir in the chocolate, kidney beans and coriander and season with salt and pepper, then leave to stand for 10 minutes.

5. Serve with guacamole, salsa, soured cream, grated cheese, tortilla chips and pickled chillies.

COOK'S TIPS

• *Instead of a can of tomatoes with garlic, use a can of chopped tomatoes and 1 crushed garlic clove.*

• *Adding a little dark chocolate to chilli con carne brings out the flavours of this tasty dish.*

Beef Goulash

Preparation Time 30 minutes • Cooking Time 8–10 hours on Low • Serves 6 • Per Serving 726 calories,
44g fat (of which 16g saturates), 21g carbohydrate, 1.6g salt • Easy

1kg (2½lb) stewing steak
2 tbsp seasoned plain flour
3 tbsp vegetable oil
700g (1½lb) onions, chopped
225g (8oz) pancetta cubes or bacon
**   lardons**
2 garlic cloves, crushed
4 tbsp paprika
2 tsp dried mixed herbs
400g can peeled plum tomatoes
150ml (¼ pint) hot beef stock
150ml (¼ pint) soured cream
salt and ground black pepper
chopped parsley, to garnish
noodles to serve

1. Cut the beef into 3cm (1¼ in)
cubes, then toss the cubes in the
flour to coat and shake off any
excess.

2. Heat 2 tbsp oil in a large pan
and quickly fry the meat in small
batches until browned on all sides.
Transfer to the slow cooker.

3. Heat the remaining oil in the pan,
add the onions and fry gently for
5–7 minutes until starting to soften
and turn golden. Add the pancetta
or lardons and fry over a high heat
until crispy. Stir in the garlic and
paprika and cook, stirring, for
1 minute.

4. Add the herbs, tomatoes and hot
stock and bring to the boil. Stir into
the beef in the slow cooker, cover
and cook on Low for 8–10 hours
until tender.

5. Check the seasoning, then stir
in the soured cream. Garnish with
parsley and serve with noodles.

Beef & Guinness Stew

Preparation Time 15 minutes • Cooking Time 8–10 hours on Low • Serves 6 • Per Serving 526 calories, 29g fat (of which 10g saturates), 10g carbohydrate, 0.4g salt • Dairy Free • Easy

1.4kg (3lb) shin of beef or braising steak, cut into 3cm (1¼in) cubes

2 tbsp seasoned plain flour

4 tbsp vegetable oil

2 medium onions, sliced

4 medium carrots, cut into chunks

225ml (8fl oz) Guinness

300ml (½ pint) hot beef stock

2 bay leaves

700g (1½lb) baby potatoes, halved if large

2 tbsp freshly chopped flat-leafed parsley

salt and ground black pepper

1. Toss the beef in the flour to coat and shake off any excess. Heat the oil in a large pan until hot. Add a handful of beef and cook until well browned. Remove with a slotted spoon, transfer to the slow cooker and repeat until all the meat is browned.

2. Add the onions and carrots to the pan and cook for 10 minutes or until browned. Add the Guinness, scraping the base to loosen the goodness, then stir in the hot stock. Add the bay leaves and potatoes and bring to the boil. Pour over the beef in the slow cooker, cover and cook on Low for 8–10 hours until the meat is tender.

3. Stir in the parsley, season to taste and serve.

Pheasant Casserole with Cider & Apples

Preparation Time 50 minutes • Cooking Time 6–7 hours on Low • Serves 8 • Per Serving 478 calories, 28g fat (of which 16g saturates), 12g carbohydrate, 0.7g salt • Easy

2 large, oven-ready pheasants
2 tbsp plain flour, plus extra to dust
50g (2oz) butter
4 rindless streaky bacon rashers, halved
2 onions, chopped
2 celery sticks, chopped
1 tbsp dried juniper berries, lightly crushed
2.5cm (1in) piece fresh root ginger, peeled and finely chopped
150ml (¼ pint) hot pheasant or chicken stock
350ml (12fl oz) dry cider
150ml (¼ pint) double cream
4 crisp eating apples, such as Granny Smith
1 tbsp lemon juice
salt and ground black pepper

1. Cut each pheasant into four portions, season with salt and pepper and dust with flour.

2. Melt three-quarters of the butter in a large pan and brown the pheasant portions, in batches, over a high heat until deep golden brown on all sides. Transfer to the slow cooker.

3. Add the bacon to the pan and fry for 2–3 minutes until golden. Add the onions, celery, juniper and ginger and cook for 8–10 minutes.

4. Stir in the flour and cook, stirring, for 2 minutes, then add the hot stock and the cider and bring to the boil, stirring. Pour into the slow cooker and season well, then cover and cook on Low for 6–7 hours or until the pheasant is tender.

5. Lift out the pheasant and put into a warmed dish and keep it warm. Strain the sauce through a sieve into a pan. Stir in the cream, bring to the boil and bubble for 10 minutes or until syrupy.

6. Quarter, core and cut the apples into wedges, then toss in the lemon juice. Melt the remaining butter in a small pan and fry the apple wedges for 2–3 minutes until golden. Return the pheasant to the sauce, along with the apples, and check the seasoning before serving.

Curried Lamb with Lentils

Preparation Time 15 minutes, plus marinating • Cooking Time 5–6 hours on Low • Serves 4 • Per Serving 478 calories, 22g fat (of which 7g saturates), 36g carbohydrate, 0.3g salt • Gluten Free • Dairy Free • Easy

500g (1lb 2oz) lean stewing lamb on the bone, cut into 8 pieces (ask your butcher to do this), trimmed of fat
1 tsp ground cumin
1 tsp ground turmeric
2 garlic cloves, crushed
1 medium red chilli, seeded and chopped (see page 30)
2.5cm (1in) piece fresh root ginger, peeled and grated
2 tbsp vegetable oil
1 onion, chopped
400g can chopped tomatoes
2 tbsp vinegar
175g (6oz) red lentils, rinsed
salt and ground black pepper
coriander sprigs to garnish
rocket salad to serve

1. Put the lamb into a shallow sealable container and add the spices, garlic, chilli, ginger, salt and pepper. Stir well to mix, then cover and chill for at least 30 minutes.

2. Heat the oil in a large pan, add the onion and cook over a low heat for 5 minutes. Add the lamb and cook for 10 minutes, turning regularly, or until the meat is evenly browned.

3. Add the tomatoes, vinegar, lentils and 225ml (8fl oz) boiling water and bring to the boil. Season well. Transfer to the slow cooker, cover and cook on Low for 5–6 hours until the lamb is tender.

4. Serve hot, garnished with coriander, with a rocket salad.

Fruity Rice Pudding

Preparation Time 10 minutes, plus cooling and chilling (optional) • Cooking Time 2–3 hours on Low • Serves 6 •
Per Serving 323 calories, 17g fat (of which 10g saturates), 36g carbohydrate, 0.2g salt • Vegetarian • Gluten Free • Easy

125g (4oz) pudding rice
1.1 litres (2 pints) full-fat milk
1 tsp vanilla extract
3–4 tbsp caster sugar
200ml (7fl oz) whipping cream
6 tbsp wild lingonberry sauce

1. Put the rice into the slow cooker with the milk, vanilla extract and sugar. Cover and cook on Low for 2–3 hours. You can enjoy the pudding hot now or leave to cool and continue the recipe.

2. Lightly whip the cream and fold through the pudding. Chill for 1 hour.

3. Divide the rice mixture among six glass dishes and top with 1 tbsp lingonberry sauce.

TRY SOMETHING DIFFERENT
• *Although wild lingonberry sauce is used here, a spoonful of any fruit sauce or compote, such as strawberry or blueberry, will taste delicious.*
• *For an alternative presentation, serve in tumblers, layering the rice pudding with the fruit sauce; you will need to use double the amount of fruit sauce.*

Winter Fruit Compote

Preparation Time 10 minutes • Cooking Time 3–4 hours on Low • Serves 6 • Per Serving 139 calories, trace fat, 26g carbohydrate, 0.1g salt • Vegetarian • Gluten Free • Dairy Free • Easy

75g (3oz) ready-to-eat dried pears
75g (3oz) ready-to-eat dried figs
75g (3oz) ready-to-eat dried apricots
75g (3oz) ready-to-eat prunes
1 star anise
½ cinnamon stick
300ml (½ pint) apple juice
300ml (½ pint) dry white wine
light muscovado sugar, to taste
crème fraîche or thick Greek-style yogurt to serve

1. Put the dried fruits into the slow cooker with the star anise and cinnamon stick.

2. Put the apple juice and wine into a pan and bring to the boil. Pour over the fruit, cover and cook on Low for 3–4 hours until plump and tender.

3. Turn the compote into a bowl. Taste the cooking liquid for sweetness, adding a little sugar if necessary. Leave to cool to room temperature.

4. Serve the compote with crème fraîche or thick Greek-style yogurt.

TRY SOMETHING DIFFERENT
Replace the figs with dried apple rings and the pears with raisins.

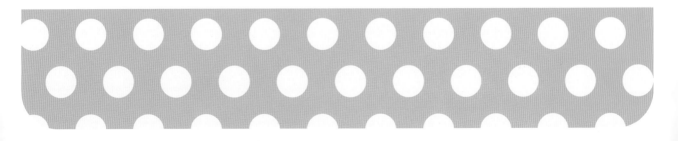

PUDDINGS

Drunken Pears

Preparation Time 15 minutes • Cooking Time 50 minutes • Serves 4 • Per Serving 305 calories, trace fat, 52g carbohydrate, 0g salt • Vegetarian • Gluten Free • Dairy Free • Easy

4 Williams or Comice pears
150g (5oz) granulated sugar
300ml (½ pint) red wine
150ml (¼ pint) sloe gin
1 cinnamon stick
zest of 1 orange
6 star anise
Greek yogurt or whipped cream
   to serve (optional)

1. Peel the pears, cut out the calyx at the base of each and leave the stalks intact. Put the sugar, wine, sloe gin and 300ml (½ pint) water into a small pan and heat gently until the sugar dissolves.

2. Bring to the boil and add the cinnamon stick, orange zest and star anise. Add the pears, then cover and poach over a low heat for 30 minutes or until tender.

3. Remove the pears with a slotted spoon, then continue to heat the liquid until it has reduced to about 200ml (7fl oz) or until syrupy. Pour the syrup over the pears. Serve warm or chilled with Greek yogurt or whipped cream, if you like.

GET AHEAD
To prepare ahead Complete the recipe, cool, cover and chill for up to three days.

Figs in Cinnamon Syrup

Preparation Time 15 minutes • Cooking Time 35 minutes, plus cooling and chilling • Serves 4 •
Per Serving 336 calories, 2g fat (of which 0g saturates), 68g carbohydrate, 0.2g salt • Vegetarian • Gluten Free •
Dairy Free • Easy

1 orange
1 lemon
300ml (½ pint) red wine
50g (2oz) golden caster sugar
1 cinnamon stick
450g (1lb) ready-to-eat dried figs
mascarpone cheese or ice cream
to serve

1. Pare the zest from the orange and lemon and put into a medium pan. Squeeze the orange and lemon and add their juice, the wine, sugar and cinnamon stick to the pan. Bring very slowly to the boil, stirring occasionally.

2. Add the figs. Simmer very gently for 20 minutes or until plump and soft. Remove the figs, zest and cinnamon with a slotted spoon and transfer to a serving bowl.

3. Bring the liquid to the boil once again and bubble for about 5 minutes or until syrupy. Pour over the figs, then cool, cover and chill.

4. If you like, warm the figs in the syrup for 3–4 minutes, then serve with mascarpone cheese or ice cream.

Hot Spiced Fruit Salad

Preparation Time 10 minutes • Cooking Time 1½ hours • Serves 6 • Per Serving 185 calories, 1g fat (of which 0g saturates), 44g carbohydrate, 0.1g salt • Vegetarian • Gluten Free • Dairy Free • Easy

3 apples, cored and chopped
3 pears, cored and chopped
12 each ready-to-eat dried apricots and figs
juice of 2 large oranges
150ml (¼ pint) apple juice
a pinch of ground cinnamon
1 star anise

1. Preheat the oven to 180°C (160°C fan oven) mark 4. Put the apples and pears into a roasting tin with the apricots and figs, the orange juice, apple juice, ground cinnamon and star anise. Stir, cover with foil and bake in the oven for 1 hour.

2. Remove the foil and bake for a further 30 minutes. Discard the star anise and serve.

TRY SOMETHING DIFFERENT
Ready-to-eat prunes or 100g (3½oz) dried cranberries can be substituted for the figs.

Rice Pudding

Preparation Time 5 minutes • Cooking Time 1½ hours • Serves 6 • Per Serving 239 calories, 8g fat (of which 5g saturates), 34g carbohydrate, 0.2g salt • Vegetarian • Gluten Free • Easy

butter to grease
125g (4oz) short-grain pudding rice
1.1 litres (2 pints) full-fat milk
50g (2oz) golden caster sugar
1 tsp vanilla extract
grated zest of 1 orange (optional)
freshly grated nutmeg to taste

1. Preheat the oven to 170°C (150°C fan oven) mark 3. Lightly butter a 1.7 litre (3 pint) ovenproof dish. Add the rice, milk, sugar, vanilla extract and orange zest, if using, and stir everything together. Grate the nutmeg over the top of the mixture.

2. Bake the pudding in the middle of the oven for 1½ hours or until the top is golden brown.

Cherry Yogurt Crush

Preparation Time 10 minutes, plus chilling • Serves 4 • Per Serving 390 calories,
18g fat (of which 9g saturates), 45g carbohydrate, 0.5g salt • Vegetarian • Easy

**400g can stoned cherries, drained,
    or 450g (1lb) fresh cherries,
    stoned**
500g (1lb 2oz) Greek yogurt
150g (5oz) ratafia biscuits
4 tbsp cherry brandy (optional)

1. Spoon some cherries into the base of each of four 400ml (14fl oz) serving glasses. Top with a dollop of yogurt, some ratafia biscuits and a drizzle of cherry brandy, if you like. Continue layering up each glass until all the ingredients have been used.

2. Chill for 15 minutes–2 hours before serving.

Summer Pudding

Preparation Time 10 minutes, plus overnight chilling • Cooking Time 10 minutes • Serves 8 • Per Serving 173 calories,
1g fat (of which trace saturates), 38g carbohydrate, 0.4g salt • Vegetarian • Dairy Free • Easy

800g (1¾lb) mixed summer berries,
such as 250g (9oz) each
redcurrants and blackcurrants
and 300g (11oz) raspberries
125g (4oz) golden caster sugar
3 tbsp crème de cassis
9 thick slices of slightly stale white
bread, crusts removed
crème fraîche or cream to serve
(optional)

1. Put the redcurrants and
blackcurrants in a pan. Add the
sugar and cassis. Bring to a simmer
and cook for 3–5 minutes until
the sugar has dissolved. Add the
raspberries and cook for 2 minutes.
Once the fruit is cooked, taste it –
there should be a good balance
between tart and sweet.

2. Meanwhile, line a 1 litre (1¾ pint)
bowl with clingfilm. Put the base of
the bowl on one piece of bread and
cut around it. Put the circle of bread
in the base of the bowl.

3. Line the inside of the bowl
with more slices of bread, slightly
overlapping to avoid any gaps.
Spoon in the fruit, making sure the
juice soaks into the bread. Keep
back a few spoonfuls of juice in
case the bread is unevenly soaked
when you turn out the pudding.

4. Cut the remaining bread to fit
the top of the pudding neatly, using
a sharp knife to trim any excess
bread from around the edges.
Wrap in clingfilm, weigh down with
a saucer and a tin can, and chill
overnight.

5. To serve, unwrap the outer
clingfilm, upturn the pudding on
to a plate and remove the inner
clingfilm. Drizzle over the reserved
juice and serve with crème fraîche
or cream, if you like.

Panettone Pudding

Preparation Time 20 minutes, plus soaking • Cooking Time 35–45 minutes • Serves 6 • Per Serving 581 calories, 29g fat (of which 16g saturates), 73g carbohydrate, 0.9g salt • Vegetarian • Easy

50g (2oz) butter, at room temperature, plus extra to grease
500g (1lb 2oz) panettone (see Cook's Tip), cut into slices about 5mm (¼ in) thick
3 large eggs, beaten
150g (5oz) golden caster sugar
300ml (½ pint) full-fat milk
150ml (¼ pint) double cream
grated zest of 1 orange

1. Butter a 2 litre (3½ pint) ovenproof dish. Lightly butter the panettone slices, then tear them into pieces and arrange in the dish.

2. Mix the eggs with the sugar in a large bowl, then whisk in the milk, cream and orange zest. Pour the mixture over the buttered panettone and leave to soak for 20 minutes. Preheat the oven to 170°C (150°C fan oven) mark 3.

3. Put the dish in a roasting tin and pour in enough hot water to come halfway up the sides. Bake for 35–45 minutes until the pudding is just set in the middle and golden.

COOK'S TIP

Panettone is a yeasted fruit cake that is a traditional Christmas treat in Italy and is most widely available around Christmas time. If you can't find it, use brioche or cinnamon and raisin bread.

Chocolate & Hazelnut Meringues

Preparation Time 25 minutes, plus softening • Cooking Time 2 hours 10 minutes, plus cooling • Serves 6 •
Per Serving 520 calories, 42g fat (of which 19g saturates), 32g carbohydrate, 0.1g salt • Easy

125g (4oz) hazelnuts
125g (4oz) caster sugar
75g (3oz) plain chocolate (at least 70% cocoa solids)
2 medium egg whites
300ml (½ pint) double cream
redcurrants, blackberries and chocolate shavings to decorate
Caramel-dipped Physalis (Cape gooseberries) to serve (see Cook's Tip), optional

1. Preheat the oven to 110°C (90°C fan oven) mark ¼ and preheat the grill. Line two baking sheets with non-stick baking parchment. Spread the hazelnuts over a baking sheet and toast under the hot grill until golden brown, turning them frequently. Put the hazelnuts into a clean teatowel and rub off the skins, then put the nuts into a food processor with 3 tbsp of the sugar and process to a fine powder. Add the chocolate and pulse until roughly chopped.

2. Put the egg whites into a clean grease-free bowl and whisk until stiff. Whisk in the remaining sugar, a spoonful at a time, until the mixture is stiff and shiny. Fold in the nut mixture.

3. Spoon the mixture on to the prepared baking sheets, making small rough mounds about 9cm (3½in) in diameter. Bake for about 45 minutes until the meringues will just peel off the paper. Gently push in the base of each meringue to form a deep hollow, then put back into the oven for 1¼ hours or until crisp and dry. Leave to cool.

4. Whip the cream until it just holds its shape, then spoon three-quarters on to the meringues. Leave in the fridge to soften for up to 2 hours.

5. Decorate the meringues with the remaining cream, the fruit and chocolate shavings. Serve immediately, with Caramel-dipped Physalis, if you like.

COOK'S TIP

Caramel-dipped Physalis
To make the caramel, dissolve 125g (4oz) caster sugar in a small heavy-based pan over a low heat. Bring to the boil and bubble until a golden caramel colour. Holding each physalis by the papery leaves, dip it into the caramel, then place on an oiled baking sheet and leave to cool.

GET AHEAD

Complete the recipe to the end of step 3, then store the meringues in an airtight container up to one week ahead. Complete steps 4 and 5 to finish the recipe.

Orange & Chocolate Cheesecake

Preparation Time 45 minutes • Cooking Time about 2¼ hours, plus cooling • Serves 4 •
Per Serving 767 calories, 60g fat (of which 37g saturates), 53g carbohydrate, 1.2g salt • A Little Effort

225g (8oz) chilled unsalted butter,
plus extra to grease
250g (9oz) plain flour, sifted
150g (5oz) light muscovado sugar
3 tbsp cocoa powder
chocolate curls to decorate (see
Cook's Tip)

FOR THE TOPPING
2 oranges
800g (1¾lb) cream cheese
250g (9oz) mascarpone
4 large eggs
225g (8oz) golden caster sugar
2 tbsp cornflour
½ tsp vanilla extract
1 vanilla pod

1. Preheat the oven to 180°C (160°C fan oven) mark 4. Grease a 23cm (9in) springform cake tin and base-line with baking parchment.

2. Cut 175g (6oz) of the butter into cubes. Melt the remaining butter and put to one side. Put the flour and cubed butter into a food processor with the muscovado sugar and cocoa powder and whiz until the texture of fine breadcrumbs. (Alternatively, rub the butter into the flour in a large bowl by hand or using a pastry blender. Stir in the sugar and cocoa.) Pour in the melted butter and pulse, or stir with a fork, until the mixture comes together.

3. Spoon the crumb mixture into the prepared tin and press evenly on to the bottom, using the back of a metal spoon to level the surface. Bake for 35–40 minutes until lightly puffed; avoid overbrowning or the biscuit base will have a bitter flavour. Take out of the oven and leave to cool. Reduce the oven temperature to 150°C (130°C fan oven) mark 2.

4. Meanwhile, make the topping. Grate the zest from the oranges, then squeeze the juice – you will need 150ml (¼ pint). Put the cream cheese, mascarpone, eggs, sugar, cornflour, grated orange zest and vanilla extract into a large bowl. Using a hand-held electric whisk, beat the ingredients together thoroughly until combined.

5. Split the vanilla pod in half lengthways and, using the tip of a sharp knife, scrape out the seeds and add them to the cheese mixture. Beat in the orange juice and continue whisking until the mixture is smooth.

6. Pour the cheese mixture over the cooled biscuit base. Bake for about 1½ hours until pale golden on top, slightly risen and just set around the edge. The cheesecake should still be slightly wobbly in the middle; it will set as it cools. Turn off the oven and leave the cheesecake inside, with the door ajar, to cool for 1 hour. Remove and leave to cool completely (about 3 hours), then chill in the fridge.

7. Just before serving, unclip the tin and transfer the cheesecake to a plate. Scatter chocolate curls on top to decorate, if you like.

COOK'S TIP
Chocolate Curls
Melt some chocolate, then spread it out in a thin layer on a marble slab or clean worksurface. Leave to firm up. Using a sharp, flat-ended blade, scrape through the chocolate at a 45-degree angle.

Chocolate Bread Pudding

Preparation Time 20 minutes, plus chilling • Cooking Time 55 minutes–1¼ hours • Serves 6 •
Per Serving 390 calories, 17g fat (of which 6g saturates), 51g carbohydrate, 0.7g salt • Vegetarian • A Little Effort

200g (7oz) baguette
100g (3½oz) milk chocolate,
 roughly chopped
500g carton fresh custard
150ml (¼ pint) semi-skimmed milk
1 large egg, beaten
butter to grease
1 tbsp demerara sugar
50g (2oz) walnuts, finely chopped
50g (2oz) plain or milk chocolate,
 in chunks
single cream to serve (optional)

1. Roughly chop the baguette and put it into a large bowl. Put the chopped milk chocolate in a pan with the custard and milk over a low heat. Stir gently until the chocolate has melted. Beat in the egg.

2. Pour the chocolate mixture over the bread, stir well to coat, then cover and chill for at least 4 hours.

3. Preheat the oven to 180°C (160°C fan oven) mark 4. Spoon the soaked bread into a buttered 1.4 litre (2½ pint), 7.5cm (3in) deep, ovenproof dish, then bake for 30–40 minutes.

4. Sprinkle with the sugar, walnuts and chocolate chunks. Put the dish back in the oven for 20–30 minutes until lightly set. Serve the pudding warm, with single cream, if you like.

TRY SOMETHING DIFFERENT
Instead of a baguette, use croissants or brioche for a richer pudding.

Cranberry Christmas Pudding

Preparation Time 20 minutes, plus soaking • Cooking Time 8½ hours • Serves 12 • Per Serving 448 calories, 17g fat (of which 7g saturates), 68g carbohydrate, 0.3g salt • A Little Effort

200g (7oz) currants

200g (7oz) sultanas

200g (7oz) raisins

75g (3oz) dried cranberries or cherries

grated zest and juice of 1 orange

50ml (2fl oz) rum

50ml (2fl oz) brandy

1–2 tsp Angostura bitters

1 small apple

1 carrot

175g (6oz) fresh breadcrumbs

100g (3½oz) plain flour, sifted

1 tsp mixed spice

175g (6oz) light vegetarian suet

100g (3½oz) dark muscovado sugar

50g (2oz) blanched almonds, roughly chopped

2 medium eggs

butter to grease

fresh or frozen cranberries (thawed if frozen), fresh bay leaves and icing sugar to decorate

Brandy Butter to serve (see Cook's Tip)

1. Put the dried fruit, orange zest and juice into a large bowl. Pour the rum, brandy and Angostura bitters over. Cover and leave to soak in a cool place for at least 1 hour or overnight.

2. Peel and grate the apple and carrot and add to the bowl of soaked fruit with the breadcrumbs, flour, mixed spice, suet, sugar, almonds and eggs. Using a wooden spoon, mix everything together well. Grease a 1.8 litre (3¼ pint) pudding basin and line with a 60cm (24in) square piece of muslin. Spoon the mixture into the basin and flatten the surface. Gather the muslin up and over the top, twist and secure with string. Put the basin on an upturned heatproof saucer or trivet in the bottom of a large pan, then pour in enough boiling water to come halfway up the side of the basin. Cover the pan with a tight-fitting lid, bring the water to the boil, then turn down the heat and simmer gently for 6 hours. Top up with more boiling water as necessary.

3. Remove the basin from the pan and leave to cool. When the pudding is cold, remove from the basin, then wrap it in clingfilm and a double layer of foil. Store in a cool, dry place for up to six months.

4. To reheat, steam for 2½ hours; check the water level every 40 minutes and top up with boiling water if necessary. Leave the pudding in the pan, covered, to keep warm until needed. Decorate with cranberries and bay leaves, dust with icing sugar and serve with Brandy Butter.

COOK'S TIP
Brandy Butter
Put 125g (4oz) unsalted butter into a bowl and beat until very soft. Gradually beat in 125g (4oz) sieved light muscovado sugar until very light and fluffy, then beat in 6 tbsp brandy, a spoonful at a time. Cover and chill for at least 3 hours.

Rich Fruit Cake

Preparation Time 30 minutes • Cooking Time about 2½ hours, plus cooling • Serves 16 • Per Serving 384 calories, 11g fat (of which 6g saturates), 71g carbohydrate, 0.2g salt • Easy

175g (6oz) unsalted butter, cubed, plus extra to grease
1kg (2¼lb) mixed dried fruit
100g (3½oz) ready-to-eat dried prunes, roughly chopped
50g (2oz) ready-to-eat dried figs, roughly chopped
100g (3½oz) dried cranberries
2 balls preserved stem ginger in syrup, grated and syrup reserved
grated zest and juice of 1 orange
175ml (6fl oz) brandy
2 splashes Angostura bitters
175g (6oz) dark muscovado sugar
200g (7oz) self-raising flour
½ tsp ground cinnamon
½ tsp freshly grated nutmeg
½ tsp ground cloves
4 medium eggs, beaten

1. Preheat the oven to 150°C (130°C fan oven) mark 2. Grease a 20.5cm (8in) round deep cake tin and line the base and sides with greaseproof paper.

2. Put all the dried fruit into a very large pan and add the ginger, 1 tbsp reserved ginger syrup, the orange zest and juice, brandy and Angostura bitters. Bring to the boil, then reduce the heat and simmer for 5 minutes. Add the butter and sugar and heat gently to melt. Stir occasionally until the sugar dissolves. Take the pan off the heat and leave to cool for a couple of minutes.

3. Add the flour, spices and beaten eggs and mix well. Pour the mixture into the prepared tin and level the surface. Wrap the outside of the tin in brown paper and secure with string to protect the cake during cooking. Bake for 2–2½ hours – cover with greaseproof paper after about 1½ hours – until the cake is firm to the touch and a skewer inserted into the centre comes out clean.

4. Cool in the tin for 2–3 hours, then remove from the tin, leaving the greaseproof paper on, transfer to a wire rack and leave to cool completely. Wrap the cake in a layer of clingfilm, then in foil

GET AHEAD
Complete the recipe, then store in an airtight container for up to three months. If you like, after the cake has matured for two weeks, unwrap it and prick it all over with a metal skewer and sprinkle with 1 tbsp brandy. Leave to soak in, then rewrap and store as before.

BASICS

Top 5 stuffings

Some people like moist stuffing, cooked inside the bird, while others prefer the crisper result when the stuffing is cooked in a separate dish – why not do half and half and please everyone? All these stuffings – with the exception of the wild rice stuffing – can be made a day ahead or frozen for up to one month. Thaw overnight in the fridge. Cook in a preheated oven, or alongside the roast.

Best-ever Sage & Onion Stuffing

To serve eight, you will need:
1 tbsp olive oil, 1 large very finely chopped onion, 2 tbsp finely chopped fresh sage, 7 heaped tbsp fresh white breadcrumbs, 900g (2lb) pork sausagemeat, 1 medium egg yolk, salt and freshly ground black pepper.

1. Heat the oil in a pan and gently fry the onion until soft and golden. Stir in the sage and leave to cool.

2. Keep 1 tbsp breadcrumbs to one side, then mix the remainder into the sausagemeat with the onion and egg yolk. Season with salt and ground black pepper, then leave to cool. Cover and chill overnight, or freeze.

3. Turn the stuffing out into an ovenproof dish, sprinkle with the reserved breadcrumbs and cook in an oven preheated to 180°C (160°C fan oven) mark 4 for 35–40 minutes until cooked through and golden.

Sausage, Cranberry & Apple Stuffing

To serve eight, you will need:
50g (2oz) butter, 1 finely chopped onion, 1 crushed garlic clove, 4 pork sausages (total weight about 275g/10oz), skinned and broken up, 75g (3oz) dried cranberries, 2 tbsp freshly chopped parsley, 1 red eating apple, salt and freshly ground black pepper.

1. Heat the butter in a pan, add the onion and cook over a medium heat for 5 minutes or until soft. Add the garlic and cook for 1 minute. Tip into a bowl and leave to cool. Add the sausages, cranberries and parsley, then cover and chill overnight, or freeze.

2. Core and chop the apple and add it to the stuffing. Season with salt and ground black pepper and stir well.

3. Turn the stuffing out into an ovenproof dish and cook in an oven preheated to 200°C (180°C fan oven) mark 6 for 30 minutes or until cooked through.

Fennel and Pinenut Stuffing

To serve eight, you will need:
75g (3oz) butter, plus extra for greasing, 1 bunch of spring onions, sliced, 450g (1lb) roughly chopped fennel, 4 tbsp freshly chopped tarragon, 50g (2oz) toasted pinenuts, 150g (5oz) goat's cheese, 150g (5oz) fresh breadcrumbs, 2 medium eggs, beaten, grated zest and juice of 1 lemon, salt and freshly ground black pepper.

1. Heat the butter in a pan, add the spring onions and cook for 3 minutes. Add the fennel and cook for 5 minutes, then leave to cool.

2. Add the tarragon, pinenuts, cheese, breadcrumbs, eggs, lemon zest and juice. Season with salt and ground black pepper and mix well. Cover and chill in the fridge overnight, or freeze.

3. Turn the stuffing out into a buttered ovenproof dish and cook in an oven preheated to 200°C (180°C fan oven) mark 6 for 30–40 minutes until golden.

Wild Rice & Cranberry Stuffing

To serve six to eight, you will need:
125g (4oz) wild rice, 225g (8oz) streaky bacon rashers, cut into short strips, 2 medium red onions (total weight about 225g/8oz), finely chopped, 75g (3oz) dried cranberries, 1 medium egg, beaten, salt and freshly ground black pepper and butter to grease.

1. Put the rice into a pan and cover with 900ml (1½ pints) cold water. Add ¼ tsp salt and bring to the boil. Reduce the heat and simmer, partly covered, for 45 minutes or until the rice is cooked. Drain and leave to cool.

2. Heat a large frying pan, add the bacon and dry-fry, turning from time to time, until lightly browned. Remove the bacon with a slotted spoon and transfer to a bowl. (If you have the goose liver, cook it in the same pan for 2–3 minutes, leave to cool, then chop it finely and add it to the bacon.) Add the onions to the frying pan and cook over a low heat until soft and translucent. Add the cranberries and cook for 1–2 minutes, then add the mixture to the bacon and leave to cool completely.

3. Add the cooked rice and the egg to the bacon mixture. Season with salt and ground black pepper, then stir thoroughly to combine. Cover and chill overnight.

4. Wrap the stuffing in a buttered piece of foil and cook in an oven preheated to 200°C (180°C fan oven) mark 6 for 30–40 minutes.

Herbed Bread Stuffing

To serve eight, you will need:
75g (3oz) butter, plus extra to dot, 1 finely chopped onion, 500g (1lb 2oz) fresh white breadcrumbs, 1 tbsp dried mixed herbs, 500ml (17fl oz) vegetable stock, 8 tbsp finely chopped fresh mixed herbs, such as parsley, thyme, sage and mint, plus extra to garnish, 2 finely chopped, celery sticks, 2 Bracburn apples, skin on, cored and finely diced, 1 tbsp ready toasted and chopped hazelnuts and 4 smoked, streaky bacon rashers (optional), salt and freshly ground black pepper.

1. Heat the butter in a large frying pan, add the onion and cook gently for 10 minutes or until softened. Stir in the breadcrumbs and mix to combine. Next, add the dried herbs and pour in the stock.

2. Mix in the fresh herbs, celery, apples and hazelnuts and check the seasoning (don't stir too much or the mixture might go gluey). Put 500g (1lb 2oz) of the stuffing for the turkey to one side.

3. Spoon the remaining stuffing into an ovenproof serving dish (add some extra stock if you like your stuffing looser) and dot with some butter. Lay the bacon strips on top, if you like.

4. Cook in an oven preheated to 190°C (170°C fan oven) mark 5 for 30 minutes until the bacon is crisp and the stuffing is piping hot. Garnish with extra chopped herbs.

SAVE EFFORT

Prepare the stuffing to the end of step 2 up to 5 hours ahead. Put the 500g (1lb 2oz) for the turkey to one side. With the remaining stuffing, either complete the recipe to the end of step 3, then cover and chill, or form into balls, wrap in streaky bacon and put on a baking tray. Cover and chill. Complete step 4 to serve.

Making stock

Good stock can make the difference between a good soup and a great one. It also gives depth of flavour to many dishes. There are four main types of stock: vegetable, meat, chicken and fish.

Meat Stock

For 900ml (1½ pints), you will need:
450g (1lb) each beef bones and stewing beef, 1 onion, 2 celery sticks and 1 large carrot, sliced, 1 bouquet garni (2 bay leaves, a few thyme sprigs, 1 small bunch of parsley), 1 tsp black peppercorns, ½ tsp salt.

1. Preheat the oven to 220°C (200°C fan oven) mark 7. Put the beef and bones into a roasting tin and roast for 30–40 minutes, turning now and again, until they are well browned.

2. Put the bones into a large pan with the remaining ingredients and add 2 litres (3½ pints) cold water. Bring slowly to the boil and skim the surface.

3. Partially cover the pan and simmer for 4–5 hours. Adjust the seasoning if necessary. Strain through a muslin-lined sieve into a bowl and cool quickly. Degrease (see opposite) before using.

Chicken Stock

For 1.2 litres (2 pints), you will need:
1.6kg (3½lb) chicken bones, 225g (8oz) each onions and celery, sliced, 150g (5oz) chopped leeks, 1 bouquet garni (2 bay leaves, a few thyme sprigs, 1 small bunch of parsley), 1 tsp black peppercorns, ½ tsp salt.

1. Put all the ingredients into a large pan and add 3 litres (5¼ pints) cold water. Bring slowly to the boil and skim the surface.

COOK'S TIPS

- *To get a clearer liquid when making fish, meat or poultry stock, strain the cooked stock through four layers of muslin in a sieve.*
- *Stock will keep for three days in the refrigerator. If you want to keep it for a further three days, transfer it to a pan and reboil gently for five minutes. Cool, put in a clean bowl and chill for a further three days.*
- *When making meat or poultry stock, make sure there is a good ratio of meat to bones. The more meat you use, the more flavour the stock will have.*

Stocks

Vegetable Stock

For 1.2 litres (2 pints), you will need:
225g (8oz) each onions, celery, leeks and carrots, chopped, 1 bouquet garni (2 bay leaves, a few thyme sprigs, 1 small bunch of parsley), 10 black peppercorns, ½ tsp salt.

1. Put all the ingredients into a large pan and add 1.7 litres (3 pints) cold water. Bring slowly to the boil and skim the surface.

2. Partially cover the pan and simmer for 30 minutes. Adjust the seasoning if necessary. Strain the stock through a fine sieve into a bowl and leave to cool.

2. Partially cover the pan and simmer gently for 2 hours. Adjust the seasoning if necessary.

3. Strain the stock through a muslin-lined sieve into a bowl and cool quickly. Degrease (see right) before using.

Fish Stock

For 900ml (1½ pints), you will need: **900g (2lb) fish bones and trimmings, washed, 2 carrots, 1 onion and 2 celery sticks, sliced, 1 bouquet garni (2 bay leaves, a few thyme sprigs, 1 small bunch of parsley), 6 white peppercorns, ½ tsp salt.**

1. Put all the ingredients into a large pan and add 900ml (1½ pints) cold water. Bring slowly to the boil and skim the surface.

2. Partially cover the pan and simmer gently for 30 minutes. Adjust the seasoning if necessary.

3. Strain through a muslin-lined sieve into a bowl and cool quickly. Fish stock tends not to have much fat in it and so does not usually need to be degreased. However, if it does seem to be fatty, you will need to remove this by degreasing it (see right).

Degreasing stock

Meat and poultry stock needs to be degreased. (Vegetable stock does not.) You can mop the fat from the surface using kitchen paper, but the following methods are easier and more effective. There are three main methods that you can use: ladling, pouring and chilling.

1. Ladling While the stock is warm, place a ladle on the surface. Press down and allow the fat floating on the surface to trickle over the edge until the ladle is full. Discard the fat, then repeat until all the fat has been removed.

2. Pouring For this you need a degreasing jug or a double-pouring gravy boat, which has the spout at the base of the vessel. When you fill the jug or gravy boat with a fatty liquid, the fat rises. When you pour, the stock comes out while the fat stays behind in the jug.

3. Chilling This technique works best with stock made from meat, as the fat solidifies when cold. Put the stock in the refrigerator until the fat becomes solid, then remove the pieces of fat using a slotted spoon.

Preparing & cooking meat

Beef, lamb, pork, ham and game such as rabbit and venison make wonderfully hearty one-pot meals, and are easy to prepare and cook when you know how. For perfectly cooked meat, choose the appropriate method for the cut. Tender cuts need quick cooking, such as grilling, whereas tougher cuts benefit from slower cooking, such as pot-roasting.

Trimming meat

Trim away excess fat, leaving no more than 5mm (¼in) on steaks, chops and roasting cuts – a little fat will contribute juiciness and flavour. When preparing meat for cutting into chunks, try to separate the individual muscles, which can be identified by the sinews running between each muscle.

Marinades

Meat is good for marinating, either wet or dry, because its large surface area allows maximum exposure to the marinade. Marinate small pieces of meat for at least 8 hours, and thick joints for 24 hours.

Wet marinades

These almost always contain some form of acid, which has a modest tenderising effect (especially in thin cuts such as steak). Before cooking, dry marinated meat thoroughly to remove liquid from the surface, and cook the marinade (skimming off the oil if necessary) as a sauce or deglazing liquid.

Dry marinades

These are useful for roasts and pot roasts. They don't penetrate far into the meat, but give an excellent flavour on and just under the crust. Make them with crushed garlic, dried herbs or spices, and plenty of freshly ground black pepper. Rub into the meat and marinate for at least 30 minutes or up to 8 hours.

GOOD ADDITIONS TO WET MARINADES

- Onions and shallots, chopped or sliced
- Asian spices, such as Chinese five-spice powder and star anise
- Chilli
- Sherry or sherry vinegar
- Brandy

Stir-frying

Perfect for tender cuts of meat.

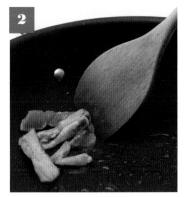

1. Trim the fat, then cut the meat into strips or dice no thicker than 5mm (¼in).

2. Heat a wok or large pan until hot and add oil to coat the inside. Add the meat and cook, stirring. Set aside. Cook the other ingredients you are using (such as vegetables and flavourings). Return the meat to the wok for 1–2 minutes to heat through.

Braising and pot-roasting

Tougher cuts of meat (see right) require slow cooking. Braises and pot roasts are similar, but braises need more liquid.

To serve 6, you will need:
3 tbsp olive oil, 1.1kg (2½lb) meat, cut into large chunks, or 6 lamb shanks, 1 large onion, 3 carrots, 3 celery sticks, all thickly sliced, 2 garlic cloves, crushed, 2 x 400g cans chopped tomatoes, 150ml (¼ pint) white wine, salt and ground black pepper, 2 bay leaves.

1. Preheat the oven to 170°C (150°C fan oven) mark 3. Heat the oil in a large flameproof casserole and lightly brown the meat all over, in two or three batches. Remove from the pan; set aside. Add the onion, carrots, celery and garlic and cook until beginning to colour, then add the meat, tomatoes and wine.

2. Stir well, season and add the bay leaves. Bring to the boil, cover, and transfer to the oven for 2 hours or until tender. Skim off fat if necessary.

PERFECT BRAISING AND POT-ROASTING

• Good cuts of beef include shin, chuck, blade, brisket and flank; good cuts of lamb include leg, shoulder, neck, breast and shank; good cuts of pork include shoulder, hand, spring, belly and loin.
• Cuts you would normally roast can also be casseroled. These simply need less time in the oven.
• Always use a low heat, and check regularly to make sure that there is enough liquid to keep the meat from catching on the casserole.
• Braises often improve by being cooked in advance and then gently reheated before serving. If you've braised a whole piece of meat, you can slice it before reheating.

Preparing & cooking poultry

From the simplest, healthiest stir-frying, steaming and poaching to the more robust pot-roasting and casseroling, there are numerous ways to make the most of the delicate taste of poultry.

Jointing

You can buy pieces of chicken in a supermarket or from a butcher, but it is more economical to joint a whole bird yourself. Use the wing tips and bones to make stock (see page 224).

1. Using a sharp meat knife with a curved blade, cut out the wishbone and remove the wings in a single piece. Remove the wing tips.

2. With the tail pointing towards you and breast side up, pull one leg away and cut through the skin between leg and breast. Pull the leg down until you crack the joint between the thigh bone and ribcage. Cut through that joint, then cut through the remaining leg meat. Repeat on the other side.

3. To remove the breast without any bone, make a cut along the length of the breastbone. Gently teasing the flesh away from the ribs with the knife, work the blade down between the flesh and ribs of one breast and cut it off neatly. (Always cut in, towards the bone.) Repeat on the other side.

4. To remove the breast with the bone in, make a cut along the full length of the breastbone. Using poultry shears, cut through the breastbone, then cut through the ribcage following the outline of the breast meat. Repeat on the other side. Trim off any flaps of skin or fat.

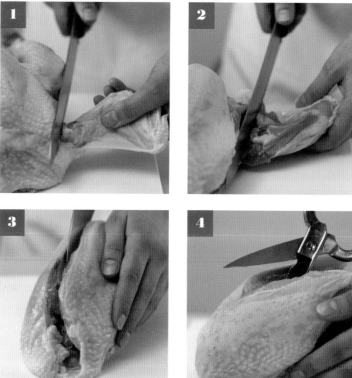

Casseroling

To serve 4–6, you will need:
**1 chicken, jointed (see opposite),
3 tbsp oil, 1 onion, chopped,
2 garlic cloves, crushed, 2 celery
sticks, chopped, 2 carrots,
chopped, 1 tbsp plain flour, 2 tbsp
chopped tarragon or thyme,
chicken stock and/or wine, salt
and pepper.**

1. Preheat the oven to 180°C
(160°C fan oven) mark 4. Cut the
chicken legs and breasts in half.

2. Heat the oil in a flameproof
casserole and brown the chicken
all over. Remove and pour off the
excess oil. Add the onion and
garlic and brown for a few minutes.

Add the vegetables, then stir in
the flour and cook for 1 minute.
Add the herbs and season. Add
the chicken and pour in stock
and/or wine to come three-quarters
of the way up the poultry. Cook
for 1–1½ hours.

Pot-roasting

To serve 4–6, you will need:
**2 tbsp vegetable oil, 1 onion, cut
into wedges, 2 rashers rindless
streaky bacon, chopped, 1.4–1.6kg
(3–3½lb) chicken, 2 small turnips,
cut into wedges, 6 carrots, halved,
1 garlic clove, crushed, bouquet
garni (see page 17), 600ml (1 pint)
chicken stock, 100ml (3½fl oz) dry
white wine, small handful of
parsley, chopped, salt and pepper.**

1. Preheat the oven to 200°C
(180°C fan oven) mark 6. Heat the
oil in a flameproof casserole. Fry
the onion and bacon for 5 minutes.
Set aside. Add the chicken, brown
all over for 10 minutes, then set
aside. Fry the turnips, carrots and
garlic for 2 minutes, then add the
bacon, onion and chicken.

2. Add the bouquet garni, stock,
wine and season. Bring to the
boil and transfer to the oven.
Cook, basting now and then
for 1 hour 20 minutes or until
the juices run clear. Lift out the
chicken, then stir parsley into
the liquid and carve the chicken.

Poaching

This gentle method of cooking will
produce a light broth.

1. Brown the bird in oil if you like
(this is not necessary but will give a
deeper flavour), then transfer to a
pan that will hold it easily: a large
frying pan or sauté pan is good for
pieces, a flameproof casserole for
a whole bird.

2. Add 1 roughly chopped onion,
2 crushed garlic cloves, 2 chopped
carrots, 2 chopped celery sticks,
6 whole black peppercorns and
1 tsp dried mixed herbs. Pour in
just enough stock to cover, then
simmer, uncovered, for 30–40
minutes (for pieces) or about
1 hour (for a whole bird).

3. Gently lift the bird out of the
liquid. If you are planning to use
the liquid as the basis for a sauce,
reduce it by at least half.

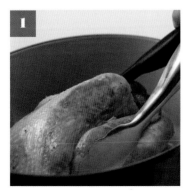

PERFECT POT-ROASTED POULTRY

• Pot-roasting is the perfect way to
cook almost any poultry or game
bird apart from duck or goose,
which are too fatty and do not give
good results, and turkey, which is
too large to fit in the average
casserole dish.
• Make sure that you use a large
enough casserole and that the
bird isn't too close to the sides
of the dish.
• Check the liquid level in the
casserole from time to time. If it's
too dry, add a little more. Water is
fine; stock or wine is even better.
• Timings for pot-roasted poultry:
about 45 minutes (for small birds
such as poussin) or 1–1½ hours
(for chicken or guinea fowl).

Preparing vegetables

The following frequently used vegetables can be quickly prepared to add flavour to savoury dishes. Onions and shallots have a pungent taste that becomes milder when they are cooked, and they are often used as a basic flavouring. Tomatoes and peppers add depth and richness to a variety of dishes. Garlic and chillies are stronger flavouring ingredients.

Onions

1. Cut off the tip and base of the onion. Peel away all the layers of papery skin and any discoloured layers underneath.

2. Put the onion, root end down, on the chopping board, then, using a sharp knife, cut the onion in half from tip to base.

3. Slicing Put one half on the board, with the cut surface facing down, and slice across the onion.

4. Chopping Slice the halved onions from the root end to the top at regular intervals. Next, make two or three horizontal slices through the onion, then slice vertically across the width.

Seeding peppers

1. Cut the pepper in half vertically and snap out the white pithy core and seeds. Trim away the rest of the white membrane with a knife.

2. Alternatively, slice off the top of the pepper, then cut away and discard the seeds and white pith.

Garlic

1. Put the clove on a chopping board and place the flat side of a large knife on top of it. Press down firmly on the flat of the blade to crush the clove and break the papery skin.

2. Cut off the base of the clove and slip the garlic out of its skin.

3. Slicing Using a rocking motion with the knife tip on the board, slice the garlic as thinly as you need.

4. Shredding and chopping Holding the slices together, shred them across the slices. Chop the shreds if you need chopped garlic.

5. Crushing After step 2, either use a garlic press or crush with a knife: roughly chop the peeled cloves and put them on the board with a pinch of salt. Press down hard with the edge of a large knife tip (with the blade facing away from you), then drag the blade along the garlic while still pressing hard. Continue to do this, dragging the knife tip over the garlic to make a purée.

Seeding unpeeled tomatoes

1. Halve the tomato through the core. Use a small sharp knife or a spoon to remove the seeds and juice. Shake off the excess liquid.

2. Chop the tomato as required for the recipe and place in a colander for a minute or two to drain off any excess liquid.

Chillies

1. Cut off the cap and slit open lengthways. Using a spoon, scrape out the seeds and the pith.

2. For diced chilli, cut into thin shreds lengthways, then cut crossways.

COOK'S TIP

Wash hands thoroughly after handling chillies – the volatile oils will sting if accidentally rubbed into your eyes.

Cooking vegetables

Nutritious, mouthwatering and essential to a healthy diet – vegetables are ideal for adding to one-pot dishes.

Stir-frying

Stir-frying is perfect for non-starchy vegetables, as the quick cooking preserves their colour, freshness and texture.

To serve 4, you will need:
450g (1lb) vegetables, 1–2 tbsp vegetable oil, 2 garlic cloves, crushed, 2 tbsp soy sauce, 2 tsp sesame oil.

1. Put the vegetables into even-sized pieces. Heat the oil in a large wok or frying pan until smoking-hot. Add the garlic and cook for a few seconds, then remove and set aside.

2. Add the vegetables to the wok, and toss and stir them. Keep them moving constantly as they cook, which will take 4–5 minutes.

3. When the vegetables are just tender, but still with a slight bite, turn off the heat. Put the garlic back into the wok and stir well. Add the soy sauce and sesame oil, toss and serve.

PERFECT STIR-FRYING

- Cut everything into small pieces of uniform size so that they cook quickly and evenly.
- If you're cooking onions or garlic with the vegetables, don't keep them over a high heat for too long or they will burn.
- Add liquids towards the end of cooking, so they don't evaporate.

Braising

1. Prepare the vegetables (see Perfect braising below). Pack tightly in an ovenproof dish. Preheat the oven to 180°C (160°C fan oven) mark 4. Dot generously with butter and season with salt.

2. Pour in stock to come halfway up the vegetables. Cover and bake for 30–40 minutes until the vegetables are soft. Baste them with the buttery stock a few times during cooking.

Stewing

1. Cut the vegetables into large, bite-sized pieces, no more than about 5cm (2in) square. Put them into a heatproof casserole (for oven cooking) or a heavy-based pan (for hob cooking). Add salt and pepper and flavourings if you like (see Perfect stews right), and mix well.

2. Preheat the oven to 180°C (160°C fan oven) mark 4 if you are cooking in the oven.

3. Pour in stock to come about three-quarters of the way up the vegetables. Cover the dish with a lid or foil and cook for 30–40 minutes until the vegetables are tender but not disintegrating.

4. Turn the vegetables once during cooking, and baste with the juices a few times.

PERFECT STEWS

• Any vegetable can be stewed; be careful not to overcook it.
• Ideal flavourings for stewed vegetables include garlic, shallots, curry powder (or Indian spices), and chilli sauce or chopped chilli.
• Potatoes will thicken the dish a little as they release some of their starch.

PERFECT BRAISING

• Carrots, fennel, leeks, celeriac, celery and cabbage are good braised.
• Leave vegetables whole or cut into chunks. Shred cabbage, then fry lightly before braising.
• Cook the vegetables in a single layer.

Preparing & cooking fruit

Most fruits taste marvellous raw, although a few always need to be cooked. Nearly all fruits make superb desserts when they are baked, poached or stewed.

Classic Poached Pears

To serve 4, you will need:
300g (11oz) sugar, 4 ripe pears, juice of 1 lemon.

1. Put the sugar in a large measuring jug and fill with cold water to make 1 litre (1¾ pints). Transfer to a pan and heat gently, stirring now and then, until the sugar has dissolved.

2. Peel and halve the pears, and toss gently with lemon juice.

3. Pour the sugar syrup into a wide-based pan and bring to a simmer. Put in the pears, cut sides down. They should be completely covered with syrup: add a little more syrup if necessary.

4. Simmer the fruit very gently for 30–40 minutes until the pears are soft when pierced with a knife. Serve hot, warm or cold.

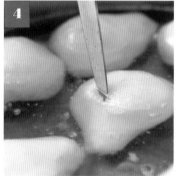

Stewing

To serve 4, you will need:
450g (1lb) prepared fruit (chunks of apples and rhubarb, whole gooseberries, halved plums), sugar to taste, 1 tbsp lemon juice.

1. Put the fruit in a non-stick stainless-steel pan with the sugar. Add the lemon juice and 2 tbsp water. Bring to the boil over a medium heat, then turn down the heat and simmer gently, partly covered, until the fruit is soft, stirring often.

Baking

The key to success when baking fruit is in keeping the cooking time short, so that the delicate flesh of the fruit doesn't break down completely. Preheat the oven to 200°C (180°C fan oven) mark 6.

1. Prepare the fruit and put in a single layer in a greased baking dish or individual dishes. Put a splash of water in the bottom of the dish(es). (For extra flavour, you can use fruit juice or wine instead of water, if you prefer.) Sprinkle with sugar (and other flavourings such as spices, citrus zest or vanilla, if you like). Dot with butter.

2. Bake the fruit until just tender when pierced with a knife or skewer: this should take 15–25 minutes depending on the fruit and the size of the pieces. Leave to rest for a few minutes before serving.

GOOD FRUITS FOR BAKING

Fruit	Preparation
Apples (dessert or cooking)	Cored and halved or quartered
Apricots	Whole, or halved and stoned
Bananas	Peeled and halved, or in their skins
Berries	Whole
Nectarines and peaches	Halved and stoned
Pears	Cored and halved or quartered
Pineapple	Cored and cut into large chunks
Plums	Whole, or halved and stoned

EASY ZESTING

• To use a zester, press the blade into the citrus skin and run it along the surface to take off long shreds.
• To use a grater, rub the fruit over the grater, using a medium pressure to remove the zest without taking off the white pith as well.

Zesting citrus fruits

Citrus zest is an important flavouring and is simple to prepare.

1. Wash and thoroughly dry the fruit. Using a vegetable peeler or small sharp knife, cut away the zest (the coloured outer layer of skin), taking care to leave behind the bitter white pith. Continue until you have removed as much as you need.

2. Stack the slices of zest on a board and shred or dice as required using a sharp knife.

Using a slow cooker

A slow cooker is perfect for the cook with a busy lifestyle. We relish the stews and casseroles our grandmothers would have dished up for a midweek supper without a second thought, but now they're a treat for the weekend when we have more time to prepare them. However, a slow cooker solves that problem: switch it on as you leave in the morning and you'll return home at the end of the day to a delicious, home-cooked meal.

What is a slow cooker and how does it work?

A slow cooker is a standalone electrical appliance, designed to be plugged in and left gently cooking unsupervised for hours, without burning or drying up the food. It consists of a lidded round or oval earthenware or ceramic pot that sits in a metal housing containing the heating element, which heats the contents to a steady temperature of around 100°C. Little steam can escape and it condenses in the lid, forming a seal that keeps the temperature constant and the food moist. It also means that a suet pudding can be left to cook for hours without needing to top up the water.

Depending on the model, there are two or three cooking settings (Low, Medium and High) and a Keep Warm function. These settings give you the option to cook a dish on High for just a few hours or on Low all day or overnight. Multi-functional models can also be used as rice cookers and steamers. Older-style slow cookers have a fixed pot to contain the food, but, nowadays, most contain a removable, dishwasher-friendly pot that can be taken straight to the table for serving.

Want to save on washing up? Choose a removable pot that can be used to start off the dish on the hob then transferred to the slow cooker unit. Alternatively, use slow cooker liners (available from specialist websites) if you have a fixed pot cooker.

Choosing a slow cooker

Anyone can use a slow cooker: some models are ideal for large families or the cook who likes to stock up the freezer, while smaller versions are suitable for couples or for students living in a bedsit. Otherwise, choose yours according to what you most like to cook: are you only planning to use it for casseroles, will you want to cook a whole chicken or are you hoping to make plenty of steamed puddings? Make sure you check the size before you buy.

What you can cook in a slow cooker

Practically anything! Don't just stick to soups, stews and casseroles. You can steam suet puddings (a brilliant hob-space saver at Christmas time), braise joints of meat and whole chickens and even bake cakes and make pâtés. Set it to cook overnight and you can enjoy a bowl of warming porridge for breakfast too. Cooking food in a slow cooker has many benefits: flavours have time to develop and even the toughest of cuts of meat become incredibly tender. It's important to raise the temperature quickly to destroy harmful bacteria so, either bring the food to boiling point on the hob first or preheat the slow cooker – always follow the manufacturer's instructions.

What you can't cook in a slow cooker

Not much! But obviously very large joints of meat and poultry such as turkey aren't suitable, while roasts and stir-fries are out of the question. Some foods, such as pasta, rice, fish, puddings and cakes, are only suitable for shorter slow cooking times so always check the recipe. Milk and cream will separate if cooked for a long time – add them to finish off and enrich a dish in the last few minutes or so of cooking time. Always fully immerse potatoes to stop them blackening while cooking.

Saving money with a slow cooker

Not only are slow cookers practical, they're economical, too, because:

• Tougher cuts of meat, such as oxtail, shin of beef or lamb shanks tend to be cheaper and benefit from long, slow cooking at low temperatures. Perfect for the slow cooker.

• It uses far less energy than a conventional oven because you are only heating up a small piece of equipment that runs on a minute amount of power in comparison.

• They're ideal for flexible meal times, saving you cash and conserving energy. It's especially useful for large active families who eat at different times – prepare one dish then keep it warm in the pot for up to two hours.

SLOW COOKER SAFETY TIPS

• Always stand the appliance on a heat-resistant surface.

• Do not use a slow cooker to reheat cold or frozen food – the temperature rises too slowly to kill harmful bacteria. Heat first on the hob then transfer to the slow cooker pot.

• Always use oven gloves to remove the pot from the slow cooker.

• Never immerse the outer housing in water; stand on a draining board to clean and remove the flex if possible.

• Never fill the outer housing with food; always use the inner pot.

• Don't let young children touch the slow cooker – the housing and the lid can become hot or spit boiling water.

• Be careful when cooking with dried beans – for example, kidney beans need to be boiled vigorously for 10 minutes to remove harmful toxins. Do this in a pan on the hob before draining and continuing with the recipe in the slow cooker.

Index